Socio-Economic Dimensions of Forest Among the Khasis

About the Author

Rekha M. Shangpliang is at present Assistant Professor at the Department of Sociology, North Eastern Hill University, Shillong. Her main research interests concern the Politics of Ecology, Indigenous Forest Livelihoods and Sociology of Environment. Her previous book is entitled "Forest in the Life of the Khasis" which was published in 2010 and she also has a number of articles and papers in academic journals and edited volumes.

Socio-Economic Dimensions of Forest Among the Khasis

REKHA M. SHANGPLIANG

CONCEPT PUBLISHING COMPANY PVT. LTD.,
NEW DELHI-110059

ISBN-13 : 978-81-8069-964-1

First Published 2013

Published and Printed by

Concept Since 1974

Concept Publishing Company Pvt. Ltd.
A/15-16, Commercial Block, Mohan Garden
New Delhi-110059 (India)
T: 25351460, 25351794, *F*: 091-11-25357109
E: publishing@conceptpub.com, W: www.conceptpub.com
Editorial Office: H-13, Bali Nagar, New Delhi-110 015, India.

Cataloging in Publication Data--*Courtesy:* D.K. Agencies (P) Ltd. <docinfo@dkagencies.com>

Shangpliang, Rekha M.
Socio-economic dimensions of forest among the Khasis / Rekha M. Shangpliang.
p. cm.
Includes bibliographical references (p.) and index.
ISBN 9788180699641

1. Community forests—India—United Khāsi-Jaintia Hills. 2. Forest ecology India—United Khāsi Jaintia Hills. 3. Khāsi (Indic people)—Social life and customs. 4. Khasi (Indic people)—Economic conditions. 5. Human ecology—India—United-Khāsi-Jaintia Hills. 6. Forests and forestry—Social aspects—India—United Khāsi-Jaintia Hills. 7. Forests and forestry—Economic aspects—India—United Khāsi-Jaintia Hills. I. Title.

DDC 333.750899593 23

पूर्वोत्तर–पर्वतीय विश्वविद्यालय
North-Eastern Hill University
Shillong 793 002, India

आचार्य अमर नाथ राय
Professor A.N. Rai
कुलपति
Vice-Chancellor

FOREWORD

I am happy to write this short Foreword for the book entitled "Socio-economic Dimensions of Forest Among the Khasis". The book is authored by Dr. Rekha M. Shangpliang.

Human beings are an integral part of the nature and their activities are conditioned by the natural environment. At the same time, human activities also have an impact on nature. The Khasis of Meghalaya had maintained a particularly close relationship with the environment in general and the forest in particular since time immemorial. Forest and forest products play an important role in the social, cultural and religious activities of the Khasis. Khasis are known for maintaining sacred groves which play an important role in conservation of species as well as a source for medicinal plants used in folk medicine.

This book by Dr. Shangpliang covers, rather comprehensively, various aspects of the relationship between forest, environment and the Khasis. The book has nine chapters covering such aspects as origin and history of Khasis, their relationship with forest, history of forest from colonial period till now and also the activities of the Forest Department. In addition, she has included original field work done by her as sample survey on two villages to analyse the socio-economic condition of Khasis *vis-à-vis* the natural resource management policy.

I congratulate Dr. Shangpliang for this work and I do hope the readers will find the book informative.

A.N. Rai

"Sa shisien pat kin win ki khlaw
sa shisien pat kin khih ki maw,
Kum kiwei pat ki sngi kin mih,
Da kumwei pat ka ri kan ih
Lada ngi don ki shkor ban sngew
Aiu ka kren ka Mei-Ramew"

"Once again the trees will sound
Once again the rocks will move
Like in the past the days will come
In another way the land will mature
If we have ears to listen
To what Mother Earth has to say……
—Soso than "ka Meirilung

Preface

The roots of this book go back to my Ph. D. thesis under the title "Forest in the Life of the Khasis: A Study in the Role of Forest in Khasi Socio-Economic Structure". I was able to get my first book published in 2010 which focussed on the means of livelihood of the Khasis, their land tenure system and classification of land and forest in Khasi Hills and highlighted on various parameters of forest usages in Khasi society. But over these few years of my teaching and research I have been inspired by specific themes on ecosystems on the natural world which has a role to play on the life of the people in general and tribals in particular. Therefore, it is hoped that the present volume will be useful to students, and scholars who are interested in understanding the status of forest in Meghalaya in general and Khasi and Jaintia Hills in particular. This book deals with a history of Colonial forestry in Assam and Khasi and Jaintia Hills and also throws light on the National Forest Policies and various forest legislations passed by the Government of India. It critically examines the implementation of development programmes by the state government and focuses on the aftermath suffered by forest in the process. The book attempts at assessing the impact of natural resource management policy of the government on the socio-economic condition of the people at grass-root level whose livelihood basically depends on forest.

The core content of this book is the field statistics and ground information collected by the author from two villages: Lawbyrwa and Madanïing-Syiem and their representation in structured tables, visual diagrams and photographs for data analysis and assessment of the dependency of the respondents on forest and their prevailing socio-economic condition. The findings of the research work are recorded in the concluding part of the book.

During the course of my research work I have received material, moral and academic feedbacks from a number of personalities to whom I take this opportunity to express gratitude and thanks.

First of all I thank my respected supervisors Prof. A.C. Sinha and Dr. I.L. Aier, Department of Sociology, NEHU without whose able guidance the achievement of Ph.D. degree would not have been possible for me. They will ever remain a fountain source of inspiration and guidance to me. I also express my gratefulness to my other senior colleagues at the department for constantly guiding me in my work.

The Village Headmen (Rangbah Shnong) of the two villages and all the respondents of my fieldwork have co-operated with me excellently. I am extremely grateful to Mr. Tony Marak, Chief Conservator of Forest, Government of Meghalaya and his officer Mr. Banjonson Nongdhar, the B.D.Os of Umsning and Mylliem Development Blocks and the two Gram Sevaks who extended valuable help in collecting important official information for my research work. The publisher Concept Publishing Company, Pvt. Ltd., New Delhi without whose kind help this book would not have seen the light of the day.

I thank God almighty for giving me such a wonderful family who has always stood by me in all my endeavours especially my husband Shem and my darling baby girl Abigail who was born just at the time when I got the first volume published and makes each day of my life happier just by being around me.

I mournfully remember my dearest mother who is no more with us today. I was lucky to have her accompany on my field visits and to look into my comfort, safety and personal needs. I tender my warmest love and homage to her, at this juncture, or what else can I do for her in return.

Last, but certainly not, the least, is my father who deserve my deepest regard and gratitude for his constant guidance and help throughout my research work, for being the one behind all success in my life and in my reaching the place where I stand now.

20th January, 2012 **Rekha M. Shangpliang**

Shillong

Contents

Glossary of Vernacular Terms

Bylla Sngi	— Daily labourer
Bylla Surok	— Muster roll
Ka Kper	— Homestead Land
Ka iiuh moi	— A harrow
Ka Latar	— A type of tree, the bark of which is used as ropes for constructing houses
Ka Rashi	— A sickle
Kha	— Born of
Khanatang bad Puriskam	— Khasi folktales and legends
Khlam	— Serious plague
Khlaw Shimet	— Private Forest
Khlaw Shnong	— Village Forest
Khnam	— Khasi arrow
Khoh	— Bamboo basket
Ki khlaw ki btap	— The forest
Ki Lum Makachiang	— The Himalayas
Knup	— Bamboo Umbrella, Rainshields
Kwai	— Betelnut
Kynbat Samthiah	— A particular flower the petals of which open when the sun rises and close as the sun begins to set
Dawai Kynbat	— Khasi Folk Medicine
Dieng Kseh Bilat	— Pure Oak
Durbar Shnong	— Village council where all disputes are settled
Hat	— Weekly market

Hynniewtrep-Hynniewskum	— Seven Huts—Seven Nests
Ja	— Cooked Rice
Law Adong or Law Shnong	— Protected or village forest
Law Kyntang	— Sacred Groves
Law Sumar	— Private Forest
Lei Khlaw	— Forest spirits
Lei Lum	— Mountain or hill spirits
Lei Muluk	— God of the State
Lei Umtong	— Water Spirits
Lei wah	— River Spirits
Lyngknot	— Wooden stool for sitting upon
Mawshamok	— White Stones
Meiramew	— Mother Earth
Mohkhiew	— Khasi Hoe
Myntris	— Ministers
Niam	— Religion
Nuli, Pantaro, Sohtung	— Species of trees used as a dye
Poikha poiman	— Marriage
Putharo Pukhlein	— Rice Pancakes
Pynthor	— Plains or wet paddy
Ri Kynti	— Private Land
Ri Lum	— Hilly Land
Ri-Raid	— Community Land
Rngai	— Shadow or spirit of the dead
Sapied Siej	— Sharp Edged Bamboo Stick
Sboh sem masi	— Lumps of decomposed cowdung
Sboh Sem sniang	— Pig Sty
Shang Kwai	— Bamboo Basket for storing betelnut
Shoh Kba	— Thrashing of sheaves
Shoh Maw	— Stone crusher
Shylliah	— Mats made of plaited cane
Siej lieh	— Species of bamboo out of which mats are woven
Sohpetbneng	— The navel of Heaven
Tang Jait	— A ceremony by which a new clan bearing

	the name of the non-Khasi mother is created
Tari	— Kitchen knife
Thang Shyrti	— Jhum Cultivation
Thup or Thak	— A Stake of firewood
Tiew Diengsong	— A particular flower associated with the onset of fever
Tih Shyiap	— Sand tiller
Tymmen Shnong	— Village headman
U Blei nongbuh nongthaw	— God the Supreme Being
U ryngkew U basa	— The guardian spirit
U Sdie	— An axe for felling trees and shrubs
Wait Bnoh	— Hooked knife
Wait Lyngkut	— Curved knife
Wait Sum	—. Butcher's Knife

Abbreviations

ADCs	—	Autonomous District Councils
CFOs	—	Chief Forest Officer
FAO	—	Food and Agriculture Organisation
IKS	—	Indigenous Knowledge System
KHADC	—	Khasi Hills Autonomous District Council
LUP	—	Land Use Planning
MFP	—	Minor Forest Produce
NBSS	—	National Bureau of Soil Survey
NRSA	—	National Remote Sensing Agency
NTFP	—	Non-timber Forest Produce
NWDPSCA	—	National Watershed Development Programme in Shifting Cultivation Areas
SHGs	—	Self-Help Groups
WDP	—	Watershed Development Programme
WDPSCA	—	Watershed Development Project in Shillong Cultivation Areas

Introduction

The expression 'Environment' is, perhaps, the most equivocal term in the lexicon of the English language. Many historians have not found environment easy to handle either as a concept or as a historical influence it makes upon the human existence. But the ideas of environment and 'nature' have played a major role both in the processes of history and its interpretation. The term environment, for some, represents an often harrowing array of physical elements like dark gloomy forests, climate and disease, which have effected the life of the people and helped to shape the course of history of mankind. The human being and environment are so closely inter-related to each other that it would often be misleading to try to define them separately. It is a well-established fact that in recent years the concepts of environment and its cognate elements have occupied an important place in people's consciousness, especially in the context of emerging environmental problems. Ever since our hominid ancestors appeared on the scene they became conscious of their surroundings with their various implications and attributes to the extent that they began to consider how they could alter them to their advantage.

Ellen Churchill Semple while citing the influence of environment on different stages of human history opened her book with a resounding statement declaring the supremacy of the environment, she writes—

> "*Man is a product of the earth's surface . . . the earth has mothered him, fed him, set him tasks, directed his thoughts,*

> *confronted him with difficulties that have strengthened his body and sharpened his wits, given him his problems of navigation or irrigation, and at the same time whispered hints for their solution... Man can no more be scientifically studied apart from the ground which he tills, or the lands over which he travels, or the seas over which he trades, than polar bears or desert cactus can be understood apart from its habitat."*[1]

The inevitable co-relation between the nature and the tribal people through the ages has made them an important component of the forest ecosystem, in which they maintain multipoint relationships within their habitat. They are dependent on them not only for their daily subsistence but more importantly they have a strong cultural and religious link with various elements of forest. As per the 1991 Census, out of the total tribal population of 67.76 million, 60 per cent of them were in close cultural link with the forests and some 30 per cent in the vicinity of the forests. The intimacy of the tribals with forest resources can be traced back to the Stone Age when early man discovered the knowledge of fire making out of a trifling forest element, which must have aroused his sense of fellowship with nature far beyond that of other animals. This new found skill further helped him in the process of burning forest and grassland for growing crops, as the indigenous people are known to have practiced jhum cultivation since ancient times. There must have been a continuous process of war and peace between man and environment, acts of trial and error, in his effort to wrest a living from myriad elements of nature which led, in the long run, to develop a certain sets of human behaviour which they call now the tribal culture and tradition.

Forest as a resource constitutes a central input to any long-term environmental security and development. Besides being the primary component of the environment, the forest plays a pivotal role in the determination of other important elements within the environment itself. For example, the forest influences the climate, regulates rainfall, produces erosion, loss of fertility and desertification. It preserves biomass and bio-diversity, conserves moisture in the soil and prevents natural calamities like floods and droughts. It has adverse effects also—as it offers obstacles to human progress and development, hinders communication, harbours evil elements (both man and beast), creates swamps and water-logging, produces germs, bacteria and diseases and affects genetic changes in biomass and human beings. However, in the days of primitive civilization, when human interference to nature was the least and knowledge of technology was virtually unknown and no industry polluted water and air; the forest played its fullest role on the life and culture of people who lived a simple life of hunting and food gathering. Our dependence on trees is not easy to forget. In the rural background, the importance of forests as the source of essential cooking fuel, building houses, house-hold articles and food and fodder is obvious enough. Present economic advancement does not reduce a society's reliance on forest products. The wood remains a basic raw material for construction of roads, bridges, buildings, furniture, railway slippers, electric poles, cellophanes, rayon, plastic, papers, etc. in increasing proportion.

Forest also performs irreplaceable ecological services. They assist in the global cycling of water, oxygen, carbon and nitrogen. They lend stability to hydrological systems, often reducing the severity of floods and permitting the recharging of springs, streams and underground waters. Trees keep soil from washing off mountain sides and sand from blowing off deserts; they keep the sediment out of rivers and reservoirs and help hold topsoil on agricultural fields. Forests house countless plant and animal species of current or potential value to humans requirement.

Until recently writings about the "basic needs" of the world's poor, generally ignored the fundamental importance of forests to human well-being. Describing conditions in Central India, forester R. Chakravarti writes: "It is often said that the three basic needs are food, clothing and shelter. One cannot think of food and shelter without wood, which is a more basic need. In fact, it may truthfully be said of an average villager that he is still in the "wood age" (Eckholm, 1991:157). Thus, the forests sustain the environment in which a happier and prosperous future of mankind is envisioned. It has been rightly observed "*the forests*" are "*the green gold of nature*".

This increasing realization of the multiple benefits of forests to mankind has created global concern for their protection and preservation and it has motivated humankind to formulate appropriate strategies and policies at various levels from global down to local.

The forest department of British India which was established in 1864 started its general policy of forest administration by enforcing new forest laws to its convenience, with a view to achieving systematic economic gains for the East India Company. Before, the advent of the British Rule in India there was only customary practice of exercising people's rights over forest and forest produce and it was only the tradition that prohibited people from cutting trees from certain protected forests. Today with a series of forest Acts, rules and regulations, there is increasing curtailment of the age-old forest rights of the tribal people living in and near the forests over the forest-produces.

Over the past couple of centuries the man-nature symbiotic relationship that existed in the past has eroded to a great extent due to stress and strain exercised by the one over the other. Man's hegemony over the nature to satisfy his greed for power and wealth led to disturb the entire environmental situation. Pressure of increased population, industrial growth, urbanization and infrastructural development led to mass destruction and denudation of forests. In Meghalaya the spread of modern education, advent of Christianity, inroad of outsiders and their culture and a borrowed world-view, all combined together to shatter the age old economy, culture and tribal ethos of the Khasis.

After the attainment of Statehood in January 1972 Meghalaya went headlong with economic development under various Five Year Plans. Construction of roads, buildings, dams and many other infrastructural developments changed the very landscape of the hills and valleys within a couple of decades. Construction of roads for communication and opening up of link roads to inaccessible areas resulted in easy connectivity to far-flung villages and paved the way for trade and business in timbers, coals, lime-stones and many other border products. These new developments acccelerated people's demand for timber and consequent increase in exploitation of forest.

The diarchical system of forest administration and management vested between the District Council and the State Forest Department in Meghalaya, has been responsible for weak and inefficient control and management of forest in the state. The major portion of forested areas of the state falls under the control of the Autonomous District

Councils (ADCs) by virtue of the powers vested on it by the Sixth Schedule of the Constitution. An interesting fact of the matter is that the State Forest department which maintains a team of well trained and adequate technical staff looks after comparatively a fraction of the total forest area of the State while the Autonomous District Council which has to manage and control several times larger area of forest remains utterly under staffed for want of adequate fund. This has led to inefficient management, non-implementation of forest conservation schemes and poor vigilance over its Reserved Forests resulting in large scale illegal felling and smuggling of timbers by unscrupulous traders into the neighbouring states.

All these adverse situations obtaining in Meghalaya's forest resources and environment not only proved detrimental to the natural storehouse of the Khasis but also brought about a serious jolt to their economy and traditional way of living. The end result of this human interference on the natural eco-system turned out to be more of a problem of supporting people's livelihood rather than the broader issue of global warming or climate change. For a backward and economically underdeveloped State like Maghalaya the basic problem that resulted from forest depletion is, therefore, a problem of deprivation of food, clothing and shelter to the poor instead of being an issue of water and air pollution.

While it is not the intention of the present study to prescribe measures to resolve the existing problems or to question the Government policies or judicial decisions, the primary objective of the author is purely academic that may be of interest for the environmentalists, students and scholars. In this book the author intends to focus on the traditional usages of forest products among the Khasis and their socio-cultural bond with various elements of nature as well as to examine the impact of emerging factors on their economy and to analyse the trend of changing harmony that emerged between Khasi and forest.

Concept and Scope of Terms

A brief discussion on the conceptual issues and scope of certain terms and phrases relating to forest, forest produce, forest community etc.

is considered essential before we go into the main subject for clarity and better understanding.

Forest

The term 'forest' has been derived from the Latin word *'foris'* meaning *'out of doors'*. Etymologically, it is 'a large uncultivated area of land covered with trees and underwood' (*Chamber's 20th Century Dictionary*, 1943). In common parlance, it denotes a group of trees in a closed canopy.

J.C. Willis, *Dictionary of Flowering Plants* 1951, Cambridge Press defines forest as: a closed assemblage of trees allowing no break in the overhead canopy, homogenous of one species or diversified".

The definition of forest given in the Indian Forest Records, Vol. 2, 1936, reads as, "an area set aside for the production of timber and other forest produce or maintained under woody vegetation for certain indirect benefits which it provides, e.g. climatic or protective".

A forest is generally defined as a plant community predominantly of trees and other woody vegetation grown in certain area of land. Food and Agriculture Organization (FAO) of United Nations defines forest as "land with a tree canopy cover of more than ten per cent and an area of more than 0.5 ha. According to the State of Forest Report, 2001, Forest is determined not only by the presence of trees but also by the absence of other predominant land uses. Thus according to FAO, timber and rubber wood plantations are classified as forest but fruit orchards and trees planted under agro-forestry system are categorized as other lands with trees outside forests.

The United Khasi–Jaintia Hills Autonomous District (Management and Control of Forest) Act, 1958 defines a Forest as: "Forest means and shall be deemed to be a forest, if in the area, there are reasonable number of trees, say, not less than twenty-five trees per acre, reserved or unreserved or any other forest produce growing on such area, which have been or are capable of being exploited for purposes of business or trade."

In judicial lexicon the term forest is understood according to the interpretation mentioned in that particular piece of Act or Rule as applicable on the matter of dispute in hand. Thus, an area of land recorded as forest in Revenue Records or proclaimed to be forest under a forest law or Act is described as forest. The Indian Forest Act VII 1865 which was the first formal law on forest, categorized forests into various types like 'Reserved' and 'Unreserved' forests due to which there was a constant need for a legal definition of forest to determine the exact class, the extent of proprietary rights of the State in any forest or the wasteland. They were all considered as falling under the categories and the nature of rights as declared within the meaning of respective forest laws.[2]

Forest as a subject was included in the provincial legislative list under the Government of India Act, 1935. Till the year 1976, it was a subject in the State Legislative List under the 7th Schedule of the Indian Constitution. However, it was the 42nd Amendment Act, 1976, which brought the subject of forest under the Concurrent List of the Constitution, the ordinance passed in October 25th, 1980 defined forest as any land containing trees, shrubs, pasture lands, any land whatsoever which the State Government may declare by notification to be forest for the purpose of this Act."

Forest Produce

The Supreme Court of India considered 'Forest Produce' as only such produce of trees having natural growth or products like flowers and fruits. The Court held:

> *Though bamboo as a whole is forest produce, if a product, commercially new and distinct, known to the business community as totally different is brought into existence by human labour, such an article and product would cease to be a forest produce. Bamboo mat is taken as a product distinct from bamboo in the commercial world, and therefore, it is not forest produce in the eye of the Act.*

The forest department had raised the plea that exclusion of bamboo products from the definition of forest produce would frustrate the object of the law and give unscrupulous dealers an opportunity to denude the country of the forest wealth. However, the Court rejected the plea on grounds that it would do more harm than good as it had the inherent danger of taking away the rights of tribal people to their habitat and livelihood.

The United Khasi-Jaintia Hills Autonomous District (Management and Control of Forests) Act, 1958 defines Forest Produce as: "those which are found in or brought from a forest, namely, timber, charcoal, caoutchouc, resin, bark, myrabolam. Trees, plants not being trees including grass, creepers, reeds, canes, orchids; and Skin, tusks, horns, bones, lac, silk and cocoons found in or bought from a forest. The expression, Minor Forest Produce or Non-Timber Forest Produce is deemed to include all items of forest produce except timber. The Dhebar Commission (1961), Hari Singh Committee (1967), The National Commission on Agriculture (1976) and several others have laid stress on the development of Minor Forest Produce for the benefit of tribals. In fact the National Commission on Agriculture (1976) held that Minor Forest Produce possesses the potential of an economic revolution among the tribal communities of India. The percentage collection of Minor Forest Produce (MFP) in the country varies from region to region. However, since most of them occur in remote inaccessible terrain, it appears that a small percentage is being actually tapped. Even at present, a big percentage of tribal population is being forced to eke out their subsistence by cultivation of marginal lands, shifting cultivation, over-grazing of forest areas and exploitation of trees.

Forest Communities

"Forest Communities" may be defined as those people whose existence depends on a close and ecologically sustainable relationship with the forest they inhabit. These communities have experienced a succession of forest-based movements in response to state intervention. Their habitats, the forest and its peripheries, contain the richest natural resource from which they eke out their livelihood. Agriculture is their primary source of income and the method of cultivation normally followed by them is shifting cultivation or jhum cultivation. They live a nomadic life shifting from one place to another following the places of shifting cultivation almost every three or four years.

Forest Villages

The origin of Forest Village begins from the days of British rule. The Indian Forest Act, 1878 provided for the constitution of forest village for within the forest itself the purpose of obtaining daily labourers required to work in the forest.

Methodology

A few words about the rationale of selecting the sample villages deserve to be spoken here. The survey was conducted on two socio-economically distinct groups of people—One group or section of people who live in forested village (not being a Forest Village) and primarily depend for their livelihood on forest and forest produce, and the other group of people are those who live away from forested village and departed from their traditional forest based economy and adopted new occupation and lifestyle as a result of changed environmental and socio-economic situation.

With this end in view that two Khasi villages have been selected with the following background and characteristics of each.

Village-I—Lawbyrwa

While selecting this village the following criteria were kept in mind:

1. It should be a well forested village.
2. Its economy should be forest-oriented.
3. It should be a village in a typical ecological setting.
4. Linked with motorable road.

Village-II—Madan Ïing Syiem

For the second village the following considerations were kept in mind:

1. A village in an urban setting.
2. Not necessarily a forested village.
3. Some evidence of change in the socio-economic life of the villagers.
4. Its economy not entirely forest-oriented.

Sources of Data

The system of data collection includes both primary and secondary methods. However, more emphasis was laid on the primary sources.

Primary Sources

In order to get sufficient primary information, two types of interview schedules were used: (a) Structured, and (b) Unstructured.

The structured interview schedules consisted of four types of schedules:

1. Block Schedule
2. Village Schedule
3. Household Schedule
4. Forest Produce Schedule.

The Block Schedule was used in procuring official records and useful data on forest and detailed statistical information about village population, area, literacy, industrial, agricultural, and animal husbandry activities of the two villages from the Block authorities

The Village Schedule was used for gathering facts and figures from the village Headmen, Gramsevaks and other functionaries of the village about the village administration and welfare activities done by the Village Council and other NGO's.

The Household Schedule and Forest Produce Schedule were the two most useful instruments used to procure primary data from the individual respondents of all the randomly selected sixty numbers of sample Households out of the entire population of each village. The information collected through these Schedules included respondent's activities concerning agriculture, industry, forestry, their dependency on forest, women and self-help group's activities etc. besides their personal details,

Unstructured Schedule

The unstructured schedule was concerned with personal interview with Government and District Council officials from the forest department and Block offices, Village Headmen of the two villages and a number of selected knowledgeable persons like Khasi elders, environmentalists, scholars and academics who provided me with valuable information on a wide variety of subjects associated with Khasi culture and tradition related to forest and other matters.

Secondary Sources

The secondary sources of information included Government reports, records and documents, published books, newspaper reports and journals, State of Forest Reports, Research papers published by ICSSR, North East Bio diversity Research Cell, NEHU, etc.

A Word on the Existing Literature

The available literature on human-nature relationship in general and on the role of forest in particular does not sufficiently explain the problem about the Khasi under study. Nevertheless, they have thrown some light on cases of similar kind which deserve our closer scrutiny. It was also imperative to study some of the key conceptual issues in environment that provided a background for the emergent social and economic structure and changing harmony between the Khasi and the forest.

E.P. Stebbing's work *The Forests of India* (1927) in 3 volumes is a comprehensive work on the general progress of forest conservancy in India. Chapter X of Vol. II of the book devotes its attention to forest Operations in Assam from 1871-1900. After portraying the valuable forest-covered land in the 5 districts of Luckimpore, Seebsagur, Naga Hills, Nowgong and Khasi and Jynteah Hills, Stebbing reveals that the extensive forests of the *Pinus longifolia* (*Pinus Khasya*) which were found in the hills around Shillong suffered from destruction by the owners themselves. Extensive forests of the *Pinus longifolia* (*Pinus Khasya*) are to be found adjacent to Shillong but the Lieutenant Governor regrets to learn of their indifferent treatment by those who own them. Government is unable to interfere in the management of these private forests, but the commissioner's attention will be called to the remarks regarding the condition of the forests within the station. "Giving an account of the reports of Mr. Schlich, who was appointed as the Conservator of Forests, Bengal and Assam, the author notes that the Conservator, Mr. Schlich does not appear to be very optimistic as to the possibilities of earning revenue out of the forests. He mentions that the high expenditure incurred in removing timber from the forest was one of the main problems that stood in the way of carrying out an export trade in timber from Assam at that time. He does not rule out the possibility of destroying forests by *jhuming* and forest fires and he gives a suggestion that the pine forests of the upper Khasi Hills could be easily conserved and extended if required by keeping *jhuming* and fires out of certain tracts should an increase of population necessitate them."

Stebbing's brief description of the methods of exploitation in force in the forests of Khasi and Jaintia Hills are notable. Among the many factors, he makes particular reference to the working of lime and coal for local consumption in Shillong and Cherrapunji. Thus the author realized the intensity of the problem of denudation of forests in these hills at a time when iron smelting was carried out extensively by using firewood especially along the western portion of the Khasi Hills.

As regards the question of *jhum* cultivation, the Report presented by the Deputy Conservator, Mr. Gustav Mann relates that as early as 1874-75 "measures had been taken up to put a stop to the indiscriminate burning of the forests in the Khasi and Jaintia Hills and the "*siems*" and Village Officers were made responsible for the conservancy of the sacred groves." Furthermore, the author has rightly observed that though these Forest Conservancy measures had met some success, but it faced certain problems like assuring the local people of the "temporary inconvenience" for a "future benefit". Comparing the case of Europe with that of India, he feels that though initially it is a difficult thing to change the habits of a population, the realization of the benefits of Forest Conservancy can come slowly only through education of the people.

The Delhi based Centre for Science and Environment, one of prime institutions in the country, has significantly contributed towards the process of systematic environmental survey in India. The Second Citizen's Report (1984-85) of the State of India's Environment is almost like a handbook for those who oppose 'modernism' and believe in the maxim 'progress towards a sustainable society'. Besides presenting a factual scenario of the nation's environmental situation the report gives a detailed account of the state of water, forests, dams, atmosphere, habitat, people, health, energy, living resources and agents of change. There are chapters in the Report that provide useful data, information and case studies related to environmental concerns in the country. Referring to Satellite data the report confirms that "India is losing more than a million hectares of forests every year, something that forest departments have consistently and perversely sought to deny. Everyday thousands of hectares of India's once rich biosphere slide into a vast wasteland. The wastelands cover no less than one-third to one-half of India's land mass."

A.C Sinha's work, *Beyond the Trees, Tigers, and Tribes* (1993), presents a historical sociology of forests in the North Eastern of Himalayan region analysing the physical features, natural vegetation and pre-colonial economy of the region. With two consequent chapters on British Forest Administration the author highlights on three themes: tea plantation and tea box timber, forest reserves and shifting cultivation and timber trade with special reference to supply of railway sleepers. The author also makes a practical analysis of people's resentment against increasing reservation of the forests by citing the case of the Garo movement against government reservation of forests in the 1st decade of the 20th century which makes it a significant study, being the only forest movement from the region which links it to other similar movements elsewhere in India.

Sinha has also given a historical account of the system of Forest administration starting from the colonial to post-colonial stage with particular reference to early efforts of forest utilization in North East frontier. His work reveals some interesting facts about the discovery of valuable plant species in and around the forests of Khasi and Jaintia Hills. "The famous botanist Joseph Dalton Hooker on a visit in 1850 collected 200 specimens of flowering plants and 150 ferns within ten miles of Cherrapunji. He also found 250 kinds of orchids, 150 varieties of grass and 15 species of bamboo:

> "The iron ore was collected from water beds and smelt on charcoal fires blown by enormous double action bellows. The forest-clad mountains in the North East of the Jaintia Hills rose 400 feet high. Timber cutters who fell *jarool* tree, which was in universal use of boat building, frequented these forests. Toon, red sandalwood and Nageesa (*Mesua ferrea*) were cut indiscriminately. Eaglewood was much sought after and was carried to Sylhet, where it was broken up and distilled for its fragrant Agar oil."

On the whole, A.C Sinha's book introduces the reader to the rich natural vegetation of the North Eastern Himalayan region and evokes some anxious questions like—What is the role of the traditional system of forest management and land laws in ecological preservation? What is the possible answer to the forest depletion in the light of the present concern and a mass movement for a balanced environmental preservation? The author also brings to light the two opposed notions of property and resource use as there has been a growing tendency to pair up the issue of communal control over forests and subsistence use on one hand and control of the state with commercial exploitation on the other.

S. Khongsit (1999) has done extensive work on various types of forest products and their uses in Khasi Hills. He takes special interest on the categorization of varied species of bamboo, fruits and even medicinal plants that are found in the Khasi Hills. In his book "*Hangne Tang ia U Siej*" (in Khasi language) he names about 44 varieties of bamboo (*siej*) and gives a detailed account of where they are found, their seasonal blooming time and their uses. He gives evidence to the fact that bamboo is the most useful of all forest products as it fulfils the needs of the Khasi life—"From the cradle to the grave." Giving a few examples Khongsit illustrates the role of the bamboo in the everyday life of the Khasi. A new born baby's umbilical cord is cut with the help of a "*sapied siej*" (sharp edged bamboo split) taken from a special kind of bamboo that grows in *ktang um* and that is the tradition among Khasis even today. Even when the baby is named, the Khasi make use of bows and arrows made of bamboo in their rituals. Lastly, when a Khasi dies his funeral will not be complete without the use of bamboo and other forest produces. The Khasis make use of a '*knup*.'(bamboo umbrella) to protect themselves from the heat and rain. It is a common sight to see the market area crowded with vendors carrying their products in a traditional Khasi '*khoh*' or bamboo basket. As it is customary, in every Khasi home, a stranger is welcomed by offering of '*kwai*' or betelnut and there is a special bamboo basket known as '*shang kwai*' meant for keeping handy some articles required for preparing '*kwai*'(betelnut).

Khongsit also relates the historic importance attached to bamboo and how it has played an important role in many Khasi folk tales and legends. Among the many famous Khasi legends is the legend of

Manik Raitong in which a peculiar species of bamboo called '*U Siej Khongpong*' grows in a historic spot on the top of a hill called '*U Lum Raitong*.' This peculiar variety of bamboo has its leaves and branches growing upside down which goes in accordance with the legendary figure 'U Manik Raitong' who is believed to have planted his flute upside down on the earth before he was put to death.

Khongsit also feels that bamboo has accelerated the growth of the handicraft industry in the North East and has given an alternative source of employment for both men and womenfolk in making useful items such as '*khoh*', '*knub*', '*trab*', '*shylliah*' and other items of decoration.

Ramachandra Guha's special article "Forestry in British and Post British India: A Historical Analysis" (1983) which featured in the *Economic and Political Weekly*, October 29, 1983 is a historical study of forest policies in India and its impact on the traditionally held rights of the forest communities. While defining "forest communities", Guha stresses on the "close sustainable relationship with the forest they inhabit." It is a well-known fact that forest dwellers during the pre-colonial period and even today, depend on their natural habitat in a multitude of ways. Guha relates that this dependence on forest has been institutionalized through various cultural and religious mechanisms. Citing the case of 'tribal India' Guha shows how the tribals have associated the identity of the forest with myths and legends. Guha also points out that the first attempt of the Colonial authorities towards asserting monopoly rights over the forest communities and thereby leading to consequent loss of control over natural resources was through the Indian Forest Act of 1865. He asserts the fact that the State monopoly right has been used at the expense of forest communities in the name of "national interest", so as to ensure that the country as a whole is not deprived of a 'national asset' by the mere 'accident of a village being situated close to a forest'.

Pointing out the flaws in the system of forest management in our country, Guha feels that this can be attributed to the 'uneconomic' and 'conservation oriented' approach that had so far characterized Indian forestry. But a change of emphasis was required from the earlier conservative approach to a dynamic one. The final answer to this came in the sixties with the official declaration by the National Commission of Agriculture (NCA), which put the dynamic "production" forestry for industrial wood production as one of its leading principles. Perhaps one can now safely assert that in view of growing deprivation of the traditional community rights to the use of forest produce, the Government should confine its forest development programme to the areas already declared as reserved forests and stress on intensive forest culture by filling up all vacant spaces with the reserved forests. Replacing the inferior and slow-growing species by the quick growing high yielding varieties should increase the productivity of forests.

Guha's paper also throws some light on the existing debate over the nomenclature 'Minor Forest Produce', though the commonly accepted system of classification of forest products have been into two categories—Major and Minor Forest Produce. He points out the fact that forest revenue from minor forest produce in our country has gone up from Rs. 30.3 million in 1947 to Rs. 1,279 million in 1976-77, and an overwhelming majority of it is collected from tribal forest areas.

This information presented by Guha is well confirmed by the present study where it has been found that about 60 per cent of the forest revenue of one of the selected villages came from Minor Forest Produce. However, in the case of the present study the use of Minor Forest Produce for trading and mercantile interest is not as fully pronounced as in other states of the country. Though it has been an important source of wages for the Khasi forest dwellers, it is more of a means of subsistence rather than an alternative to starvation.

H.O. Mawrie's book *The Khasi Milieu* (1981) is a compilation of some important themes in Khasi life and culture like marriage, family, religion, village, administration, folktales, etc. and he devotes two chapters exclusively to focus on the role of nature in Khasi life. His resounding declaration "A Khasi lives with nature and nature lives in him" summarises the close affinity between the Khasi and nature. Mawrie relates the symbolic significance of trees by associating them with Khasi folk tales and legends. Citing an example of the oak tree, he portrays the anthropomorphized appearance of the oak tree with its far-flung branches resembling to a strong man who never surrenders.

There are also lessons to learn from nature as in the words of Mawrie, "*A Khasi lives in nature and learns in its bosom*". Nature has nurtured them from their infancy and its every movement, every sound and every single object has a lesson to teach them. Mawrie relates some commonly accepted notions about nature's role in shaping the very life and existence of a Khasi. For a farmer, the first sound of thunder is an indication that it is time for paddy cultivation. There is also a premonition, when the moon is on the wane it is considered a bad time to cut bamboo or reeds because the finished product may not last long if cut during that time. Mawrie compares nature to a book wherefrom the lessons and wisdom learnt are useful for a Khasi in his everyday life.

Mawrie's book also unfolds the rich storehouse of Khasi folk tales and legends that centre on things and objects seen in nature. Besides the moral values attached to these folk tales, they are also an important source of information about the long attachment between the Khasi and nature that have existed since time immemorial. The famous legend of U Manik Raitong and his flute is a classic example of how the Khasi still look up to a particular species of bamboo '*siej khongpong*' that has its leaves growing downwards.

Tiplut Nongbri's book *Development, Ethnicity and Gender* (2003) which is a compilation of select essays on tribes in India reveals some startling facts about the infringement by government policies the people's rights over land, mine and forests, thereby contributing to the depletion of the country's natural resources, such as water, trees, minerals and soil. She points out the fact that this phenomenon becomes more deeply pronounced in the tribal belts of the country, because of the tribal people's high dependence on natural resources to meet their survival needs. Explaining the meaning of 'land'for the tribals, she remarks "the concept of land as property that is central to commodity based economics was far removed from the tribal conception of land. In the conception of tribes, land is not a private resource to be monopolized by the holder at will. Among many tribes land is considered to be a gift of nature, hence it belongs to the community. Accordingly, while all members of the community have rights of access to it, control over it lies with the collectivity."

Nongbri suggests an important methodological tool as a pre-requisite for any study of land and land based relations, which should involve a critical examination of the concept of "Rights" both in the legal as well as local terms of understanding. This holds truth in the

development can only be achieved in the collaboration of public policy and private initiative to this end."

Hamlet Bareh Ngap Kynta in his book *The Economy of Meghalaya—Tradition to Transition* (2001) brings out the "techno-economic character" of traditional Khasi economy, where Forest-based industries also finds mention among others like wet-rice farming, iron-smelting, excavation of metals, handloom weaving and pottery. While noting the growth of some rare and valuable species of trees like teak, champak, beach, nahar, asparagus, sal etc. Bareh also mentions about the indigenous Khasi pines which grow at an elevation between 1,500 and 1800 meters. He does not rule out the possibility of deforestation even in the past and attributes this primarily to occupations like iron smelting and blacksmithy which has been in existence since the past and is still operated in the traditional style where wood-burnt charcoal is mostly used for fuelling. In a separate chapter entitled "Trends and Transition", Bareh has listed the key issues that need proper attention in the light of a sustainable economy for Meghalaya. On the issue of forest, Bareh notes that the first step should be to take up a utility oriented planning conforming to the trend of an increasing population especially in a State like Meghalaya. One of the pertinent issues that needs to be addressed is to introduce a suitable system of land management policy, where the bulk of forests would not be privately owned and managed by individual, family or community. There should be a constant effort on the part of the government to exercise proper control over these existing private forests which will deter destruction of forests and contribute to the protection of ecological balance and maintenance of good climate and rainfall. The author expresses his satisfaction on the afforestation programmes implemented by the government and the public and proudly notes the fact that while India accounts for the existence of 1400 to 1600 species of excellent orchids, 150 species of them are found in Meghalaya State. He therefore, calls for an urgent need of saving the valued flora and fauna wealth of the State from being wantonly destroyed and depleted. Besides, he feels that there is the need to invest on raising nurseries for fresh plantations of quick growing trees which would increase the scope of economic productivity.

Tiplut Nongbri's paper "The Khasi Land Tenure System: Need for conceptual Refinement" in the NEICSSR journal *Land Relations in North East India* edited by B.B. Dutta and M.N. Karna explores the ground realities of the existing land tenure system among the Khasi and thereby brings out the socio-economic implications of unequal distribution of land and economy. She notes the ambiguity surrounding the concept of ownership, control and occupancy rights of Khasi land tenure system. Though the land tenure system presents an egalitarian picture, as the author notes, an indepth empirical study of the problem reveals that there is wide discrepancy between ideal and the actual practice. Most of the forest lands that fall within the community land or *Ri-Raid* land are subject to be misused by those having vested interest, on the one hand, and by the traditional legal machinery which makes the final adjudication, on the other.

Pointing out the loopholes of the existing Khasi land tenure system, Nongbri attributes it to the absence of a codified land tenure system where the concepts of ownership, control and occupancy-rights are supposed to be clearly defined. This confusion is prevalent in both public as well as privately owned lands. While in the case of public land, the problem is one of occupancy-right of land, which seemed to favour the rich, in the case of private land; the controversy is tied up with the Khasi rules of inheritance of ancestral property where land is unequally distributed among the daughters. Nongbri further explains that this ambiguity could be detrimental to economic development of the region in the long run. Thus she suggests an urgent need to first understand the social implications and then go for reforms because "land among the Khasi is not only a symbol of social status but also the focus of agrarian relations.

Books on Vernacular Literature

K. Dhirendro Ramsiej (1992) in his book entitled *Ka Mariang ha U Khasi bad Ki purinam-puriskam*, brings out the intricate relationship between nature and culture amongst the Khasis. A number of Khasi folktales and legends associated with nature-man relationship have been highlighted by the author which throws light on the part played by nature in shaping the Khasi culture. In a separate chapter entitled "Ka Mariang ha ka rukom pyrkhat U Khasi," the author, while talking about the influence of nature on Khasi literature, mentions the name of Soso Tham, the Father of Khasi poetry as being a pioneer in describing the beauty of nature in Khasi poetry. Nature is described as a book that teaches us the lessons of life. In short, the author gives us a vivid idea of the Khasi concept of nature and of the oneness of God, man and nature.

"*Ka Ain u Khasi*" by T. Cajee is a Khasi translation of 'Notes on Khasi Law' by K. Cantlie which deals with the land tenure system of Khasi and Jaintia hills which has a close bearing with the socio-economic system, forestry and *jhum* cultivation of the Khasi.

In the book, *Ka Dieng bad ka Culture Jong Ngi* by S. Khongsit narrates the numerous species of trees, plant and herbs that grow in Khasi-Jaintia hills which have played an important role in the life of the Khasi both in the past and present. For example, Khasi civilization begins with the tree called *Ka Tula* in Khasi (*Anaphalis griffithii*). The Khasi ancestors made fire with the dried flower petals of this tree out of the spark produced from the friction between two pieces of white stones called *Mawshamok*. He claims that some people of the village Khadar-shnong in Sohra were practicing this method till 1945 and did never buy match boxes. In olden days people used the bark of this tree called *Ka Latar* as rope for tying while constructing houses as it was considered a taboo to use nails in dwelling houses. He writes that Khasis not only weaved clothes for themselves but also knew the art of dying clothes in fast colours obtained from the bark and leaves of trees like Nuli, Pantaro, Sohtung etc. The book is an account of numerous names of trees and plants and their usages made by the Khasis. Talking about the role of theology and culture in the maturity of human civilization, H.O. Mawrie in his book *Ka Theology Jong ka Niam Khasi* stresses the importance of understanding the theology of a tribe. The author also speaks about the role played by the environment in shaping the culture and belief of humanity Man is already a part of nature as nature is a part of him. Khongsit says, the messages given by the river Ganga to the Hindus, by the mountain Fujiyama to the Japanese, by Mecca to the Muslims, by Jerusalem to the Jews, by Calvary to the Christians are understood only by them. Similarly, the Khasis have many hills and valleys, rivers and streams, sacred forests and monoliths, whose language is known to the Khasis alone. He gives an illustration of various legends, folktales etc. to explain Khasi beliefs and customs.

This book is divided into nine chapters or parts. The first chapter deals with the origin and history of the Khasis who are described as one of the Mon-Khmer speaking races akin to the Mundas of Chotanagpur district of Madhya Pradesh. It gives a panoramic description of their land and geography, hills and rivers, flora and fauna and narrates how intimately the life, culture and literature of the Khasis are linked up with the various forms of nature.

Chapter two delves deep into the Khasi concept of forest and the nature, and brings out the close relationship between them and their environment. It avers the fact that the Khasis live in nature and the nature lives in them. It speaks about the Khasi belief in eco-theandric relationship between god and the mother earth whom they call *Meiramew,* a sacred entity.

Chapter three narrates in brief the history of forest during colonial rule in Assam and Khasi and Jaintia Hills. Assam was covered with extensive forests full of deciduous hardwood trees like sal, teak, ebony, jarul, sissu, etc. which fetched high price in foreign markets. The British looked at these natural rich forest of Assam as a potential source of revenue. They introduced forest Acts and appropriated the forest wealth by constituting reserved forests where the local people were restricted to exercise their rights to enter and use the forest produces. The colonial government opened Forest department, appointed Conservator of forests, made rules for systematic conduct of forest administration and utilized the treasure of forest wealth for the benefit of the government.

Chapter four of the book deals with the post-independence history of forest in Khasi and Jaintia Hills. It highlights on the National Forest Policies 1952/1988 and the Forest Acts passed by the Government of India from time to time for conservation and development of forest resources of the country. It critically examines the implementation of various economic development programmes by government and focuses on its aftermath on the forest resource of India.

In chapter five of the book, the author describes the activities of the Forest department both during the British rule as well as after independence and attempts at assessing the impact of the natural resource management policies of the two governments on the socio-economic condition of people who are dependent on forest.

Chapter six and seven are the field work data and other ground information collected by the author on two sample villages, viz. Lawbyrwa and Madan Iing-Syiem to chart out the role of forest in the life of the Khasis and to analyse the impact of natural resource management policy of the government on the socio-economic condition of the Khasis.

Chapter eight is a comparative study of the socio-economic profiles between the two sample villages which helps us to examine the differences in the ecology of the traditional and modern villages and to determine the changes that have taken place due to impact of forest management policies of the government.

Chapter nine is the concluding remarks of the author on the findings of the research work based on the field works carried out.

Notes

1. Semple, Ellen Churchill, *Influence of Geographic Environment on the Basis of Ratzel's System of Anthro-geography*, 1911, London.
2. Sinha, A.C., *Beyond the Trees, Tigers and Tribes: Historical Sociology of the Eastern Himalayan Forests*. 1993, p. 39

1

The Khasis: People, Land and Ecology

The Khasis occupy a unique position both from ethnic and linguistic points of view among the congeries of the tribes inhabiting the mountainous region of India's North East. While opinions vary about the origin of the Khasis, one section of the historians and anthropologists hold the view that the Khasis belong to the Mon Khmer group of Indonesia and that linguistically they are related to the Mundas who are located in Chotanagpur region of India.[1]

There are numerous interpretations of the word "Khasi". Hamlet Bareh suggests that the term "Khasi" means "*born of the mother*"; "*kha*" means "*born of*" and "*si*" refers to "*ancient mother*", thus bringing out the matrilineal character of the Khasis who trace their descent from the mother.[2] The origin of the Khasis as a race is shrouded in mystery, which has led historians to give different interpretations about their history and origin.

Regarding ethnic identity of the Khasis the general finding of linguists and ethnographers is that they are by race Indo-Mongoloid although speaking a distinct Austric language belonging to Mon-Khmer group.[3] As regards the question, 'Who is a Khasi'—the Land Reforms Commission for Khasi Hills (Vol. 1) opined that a person who is acceptable as a Khasi is one whose parents descended since time immemorial from the descendants of the people inhabiting *ka Ri Khadar Doloi, Ka Ri Laiphew Syiem*, or who has adopted Khasi socio-political customs and way of life, conducts and comports himself as a Khasi, speaks Khasi language, follows a matrilineal system, and in the case of male adults have a right to take part in traditional durbars of the Khasis in a place where he lives or do take part in the election of hereditary Chiefs of his *elaka* where popular election is held in which women cannot take part and is accepted by the rest of the people as belonging to their tribe.[4] David Roy defined a Khasi as a person who is a descendant of the folk, who found a home in these hills and is governed by Khasi laws of consanguinity and kinship. A Khasi is a Khasi because of his religion (*Niam*) which regulates all his thoughts and activities.

Hamlet Bareh describes "Khasi" as a general term encompassing various tribes and sub-tribes inhabiting the Khasi and Jaintia Hills namely:[5]

1. *Khynriams* or *Nonglum* (Khasi proper) inhabiting the middle ranges of the Khasi Hills, comprising the *Khynriams* proper and their allied tribes in the central plateau;
2. *The Pnars* inhabiting the central plateau of the Jaintia Hills. The *Pnars* are also called the *Syntengs*, but they prefer to be called *Pnars*;
3. *The War* people of the south, comprising the *Shella* people and their allied tribes;
4. *The Amwi* people and their allied war, *synteng* and other tribes in the south Jaintia Hills who form apparent tribe of the present Khasi-Pnars in their earliest period of settlement in the land;
5. *The Bhoi* people, both *Khasi* and *Pnar* inhabiting the north of Khasi and Jaintia Hills with their different sub-groups (Hamlet Bareh, 1985).

According to A.S. Khongphai, the non–controversial definition of a Khasi is a person born of a Khasi mother, irrespective of the fact whether is a Khasi or a non-Khasi. However, their definition has been modified with the introduction of Khasi Lineage Bill 1997, which defines a Khasi as one whose parents are/were both Khasis and whose clan name is taken from the mother. For those born of a Khasi father and a non-Khasi mother, the Bill has invoked the old custom of "*Tang Jait*" a ceremony by which a new clan bearing the name of the non–

Khasi mother is created. The Bill further states that to be a Khasi the person will have to know the Khasi language unless prevented from knowing it by circumstances beyond his control like living outside the area. He must also observe and be governed by the Khasi matrilineal system, Khasi law of inheritance and succession and the Khasi laws of consanguinity and kinship.

In short, as mentioned by Mr. Thomas, the Magistrate of the District Council Court,—to be a Khasi, one has to live like a Khasi, dress like a Khasi, eat like a Khasi, speak Khasi Language and follow the Khasi customs and traditions. Though all Khasis have fundamentally the same language and social structure, their culture, dialects, economy, social usage and political organisation vary greatly owing to the ecological and politico-historical differences among them.

The various myths and legends associated with the origin of the Khasis provide us with ample evidence about their long period of association with Gods and heavenly beings. One such interpretation is incorporated in their legend of the *Hynniewtrep-Hynniewskum* or the Seven Huts–the Seven Nests. This legend tells the story of how God in the beginning created sixteen families and let them stay with him in heaven. He allowed them to move freely between Heaven and Earth with the help of a golden ladder which touched the top of a mountain peak name *Sohpetbneng* (The Navel of Heaven) until one day when seven of them chose to remain on earth leaving the remaining nine in heaven. From that day God removed the ladder and the seven families on earth came to be known as *Ki Hynniew Ha Tbian* (The Seven Below) and those who remained in Heaven as *Ki Khyndai Hajrong* (The Nine Above). The Khasis, as we know them today, according to their timeless tale are the descendants of the Seven Below, and they have flourished throughout their beautiful land.

The manner of migration of the Khasis is believed to be responsible for disappearance of their traditions and knowledge about their movement from the place of origin into present hills that took place in the past. The commonly accepted view is that they came from the Far East and used the same route of migration followed by other immigrants from Burma. This fact is supported by the finding of a close affinity between the Khasis and the Mon–Khmer who live in the Far East country.[6] It is also interesting to note that the Khasis appear to have a close association with the Himalayan ranges, as they have their own name for these ranges '*Ki Lum Makachiang*' which indicates that the Khasis had once settled in the neighbourhood of the Himalayas, or at the foothills of these mountains around Darrang, Sadiya and Dibrugarh.[7]

According to J.R. Logan, the Khasis have a close relationship with the Mons or Talaings of Pegu and Tenasserim, the Khmers of Combodia and the inhabitants of Aman. Logan identifies a tribe called the Palungs who inhabit the Shan States of Myanmar, as the closest kinsmen of the Khasis. In the opinion of Roy, the Khasis belong to the Mongoloid family on account of the similarity of the languages of these two groups.[8] Looking at the close similarity between the Mundas and Khasis in their rites and rituals on veneration of the dead, Walter G. Griffith was of the opinion that the Mundas who are located in the Chotanagpur area were the ancestors of the Khasis.[9]

While it is true that the Khasis have inhabited in these hills for a very long time and that their direction of migration was from east to west, many support the view that the Khasis are linguistically and racially an offshoot of the Mon-khmer branch of the Austro-Asiatic stock and are believed to be the remnants of the first Mongolian overflow into India.[10]

Land and Geography

The Khasi and Jaintia Hills are bounded on the north, east and south-east by Assam, on the south by Bangladesh and on the west by Garo Hills of Meghalaya. Until 1970 the United Khasi and Jaintia Hills was one of the districts in the erstwhile composite State of Assam. After the creation of the Autonomous State of Meghalaya on 2nd April 1970 and the attainment of full statehood on 21st January 1972, the United Khasi and Jaintia Hills and the Garo Hills District formed the constituent Districts of Meghalaya with the headquarters at Shillong and Tura respectively. Thereafter, the Khasi Hills District was divided into two districts namely the East Khasi Hills District and the West Khasi Hills District on 28th October, 1976. However, on June 4th 1992, East Khasi Hills District was further divided into two administrative districts of East Khasi Hills District and Ri Bhoi District. According to the Census of India 2001, the total population of East and West Khasi Hills was 9,55,109 persons.[11]

The land of the Khasis, (according to traditional geography) can be divided into three divisions—the *Ri-Bhoi, Ri-Lum* and the *Ri-war* which means the territories of the Bhoi people, of the Hill people and of the Plains people. The first division starts from the Ri-Bhoi region with open valleys and scattered flat lands (of the Brahmaputra valley) gradually rising in its altitude to form a compact plateau, comprising the Ri-Bhoi district. The second division of Ri-Lum consists of a number of irregular hill ranges of metamorphic rocks comparatively higher in altitude among all the hill ranges, with narrow flat basins in between them. The highest elevation of this division is the Shillong peak with 1961 meter above sea level.[12] The central plateau of Jaintia Hills belonging to this division, is formed of mostly small ranges of with extensive valleys amid them.[13] The third division called the *Ri-War*, is a vast low lying hill ranges along the southern fringes of the division which includes areas like Mawsynram, Sohra and Syndai platforms renowned for heaviest rainfall in the world. The hill ranges end up abruptly in precipitous gorges towards the south and finally terminate at the Bangdesh border around Ranikor, Lynhkhat, Dawki, Muktapur, etc.

It is interesting to note that many of the hills in Khasi and Jaintia hills are known by their specific names and are associated with Khasi legends which bear special significance concerning their race and origin, beliefs, etc. For example, the hill situated a few kilometers away from Umiam Dam-site is traditionally known as *U Lum Sohpet Bneng* (Heaven's navel peak) and is associated with the legend about the origin of the Khasis. The legend says that in the beginning the ancestors of the Khasis descended down from heaven on this hill top through a golden ladder connected with heaven. The Shillong peak, Meghalaya's highest peak, overlooking the beautiful city of Shillong bears its traditional name as *Lum Shyllong*. This majestic peak is attached with a folk-lore of a beautiful fairy queen named *Ka Pah Syntiew* who lived in a cave and in course of time happened to be the ancestress of the Syiem of Shyllong.[14] There is yet another hillock called *Lum Diengiei*, a few kilometers south of Shillong which is considered as a sacred and awe-inspiring spot, being a place where a giant tree with its branches over casting widespread shadow and darkness existed and the people cut it down ultimately after persistent hard work. There are numerous other hillocks associated with traditional legends and folk tales in Khasi and Jaintia Hills like, the *Lum Kyllang* (Kyllang rock), the *Lum Symper* (Symper rock), the *Lum Iawpaw* (Iawpaw rock), *Lum Lamare* (Lamare rock) and so on.

Rivers and Waterfalls

The Khasi and Jaintia Hills is a land of numerous rivers and streams. They take rise in the high hills and flow down silently cruising through hard rocks and crags, at times, cascading down the precipitous gorges making it a breath-taking scene of beauty and at another slowly meandering down the valleys. Most of the rivers originate from the central plateau, flow down towards the south forming deep gorges and finally join the river Surma in Bangladesh. The rivers that flow towards the south are the *Kynshi iong*, the *Umiew or Umiam Mawphlang* and the *Umngot*. The principal rivers that flow towards the north are *the Khri, the Umtrew*, the *WahUmiam* and the *Wah Umken*. These rivers ultimately join the great river Brahmaputra in Assam.

Some of the well known waterfalls are *Kshaid Noh- Sngi-Thiang, Kshaid Noh-Ka-Likai, Kshaid Dain-Thlen, Kshaid Umshyrpi* or Beadon Falls, *Kshaid Sunapani* or Bishop's Falls, *Kshaid Umdiengpun* or Elephants Falls, *Kshaid Weitdem* or Sweet Falls (*Kshaid* is the Khasi term for waterfall).

One very significant matter that is hard to escape the notice of any sentient human being is the existence of a strong sense of eco-consciousness of the Khasis about their land and natural environment.

Flora and Fauna

Perhaps the floristic composition of the Khasi Hills is nowhere commented with such appreciation as has been done by Dr. Joseph Dalton Hooker in his Himalayan Journals. Hooker's journey up to these hills in 1850 was indeed rewarding, taking into account his valuable observations of the richness and variety of the colour, form and size of each blossoming plant. In his own words, "It is extremely difficult to give within the limits of this narrative any idea of the Khasi flora which is, in extent and number of fine plants, the richest in India, and probably in all Asia, the collected upwards of 2,000 flowering plants within ten miles of the station of Churra (Cherra) besides 150 ferns, with a profusion of masses, lichen and fungi. Orchidaceae are, perhaps, the largest natural order in the Khasia where fully 250 kinds grow, chiefly on trees and rocks, but many are terrestrial, inhabiting damp woods and grassy slopes. I doubt whether in any other part of the globe the species of orchids outnumber those of any other natural order, or form so large a population of the flora".

On the whole, there can still be ample scope for exploration of plant species in these hills. However one cannot deny the Herculean efforts of plant explorers like Griffith (1847), Hooker (1854), Clarke (1889), Bor (1938, 1942), Biswas (1941, 1943), Kingdon-Ward (1960) and Burhill (1965) who have given accounts of the flora of this region. The first systematic treatment of the flora of the north eastern region is by Kanjilat *et al* (1939-40), a work in five volumes (incomplete). The first four volumes cover the Dicotyledons, chiefly the woody species being forest flora and the fifth volume by Bor (1940) deals with the Germinae only.

The establishment of the Botanical Survey of India in the country way back in 1890 made some significant efforts to create public interest in the plant life of Khasi Hills after 1956. One laudable effort of the BSI has been to work in collaboration with the North Eastern Council in launching a programme for the cultivation, multiplication, preservation and supply of orchids to collectors at a cheaper rate with a view to prevent depletion of the natural habitats.

A careful survey of the vegetation in these hills reveals some alarming facts and remarkable instances of disjunctive distribution. The discovery of novelties of very rare species have been found such as *Nymphaea pygmea* (South Siberia and North China); *Magnolia lanugimosa* (Nepal); *Hemalium schleichii* (Burma), etc. which add to the diversity of species composition in the region.

Another remarkable feature of the floristic variety of the Khasi Hills is found in the Sacred Groves located at several areas in and around Shillong Peak, Mawphlang and Mawsmai. These groves are home to some very rare species of orchids and a number of plants. A number of botanical explorations over the last 50 years have revealed that *Ilex khasiana* a small evergreen tree that grows with thick foliage in the forests of Meghalaya is facing extinction.

The National Orchidarium at Shillong maintains over 300 species of orchids of North Eastern Region and the Experimental Garden at

Umiam (Barapani) maintains the germplasm bank of many rare and threatened orchids, besides several rare, endangered, medicinal plants (Mao *et al.* 1999).

A recent survey conducted by the National Botanical Research Institute, Lucknow which is one of the premier institutes of Council of Scientific and Industrial Research (CSIR) has undertaken a project on research and development work in the North Eastern Region. Under this project, Dr. V.P. Kapoor, Head of the Plant Chemistry Division, National Botanical Research Institute reported that Meghalaya has enough dye-yielding plants which may be utilised to set up local dye producing units. It was reported that the roots and stem of a prominent plant *Rubia cordifolia* (local name Sacre) contain yellow dye and the leaves of *Camellia caduca* (Samkhi) contain brown dye. With the increasing trend nowadays for use of textile and consumer goods dye by natural dyes, there is enough potential to use these dye yielding plants for local industry and generate awareness to local people and entrepreneurs through training programmes [15]

"The fauna of the Khasi Hills is intimately connected with the geomorphological evolution of the area. This region served as a fauna gateway through which their Indo-Chinese elements of Oriental fauna and Palaearctic montane fauna spread to the main sub-continent. As a result, a complex assemblage of Indo-Chinese, Indo-Myanmar, Ethiopian and Palaearctic montane elements could now be observed" (Dr. C. Radhakrishnan, Zoologist and Officer-in-Charge, E. Regional Station, Zoological Survey of India).

The existing eco-systems are conducive to the growth of evergreen forests that are the habitat of rich mammalian fauna and other forms of animal life, mammals like the Hoolock (Gibbon) the Golden Cat (*Felis termnuckii* Vigors and Horefeld) the leopard cat (*Felis bangalensis* Kerr), the Jungle Cat (*Felis chaus* Guldenstaedt), to name a few have added a unique assemblage to the oriental fauna of the Khasi Hills.

Besides mammals, birds of various species are found in abundance in the forests specially in low altitude areas like the forests of the Nongpoh-Lailad areas in Khasi Hills. The common birds found include the long tailed Broadbill (*Psarosomus dalhousiae* Jameson), the Burmese Roller (*Coradias benghalensis affinis* Horsfeld), The Blue throated Barbet (*Megalaima asiatica* Latham), the Red-vented

Bulbul (*Pynonotus cafer bengalensis* Blyth), the Himalayan Black Bulbul (*Hypsipetes madagascariensis psaroides vigors*) the Hill Mynah (*Gracula religiosa* Linn) etc. which are only a few of the many exotic species of birds found. Reptiles and fish species of the Khasi Hills also exhibit excellent qualities of adaptation to the climate and topography of the region. Mention should be made about the exotic species of butterflies like the Blue Peacock, the orange oak leaf and the Bhutan Glory that add to the interesting assemblage of insects in the region.

According to official reports on the faunal resources in the seven sisters states of the North East, 650 species of plants and 70 species of animals who find a habitat in the region have been listed as endangered due to human depredation, poaching and other non-planned and non-forestry activities[16] While there is a concerted effort to preserve the fragile eco-system in the region which has been identified as one of the 18 'hot spot' areas in the world with reference to threats to the rich bio-diversity. What is of serious concern today is the fact that there is a lack of positive activity on the part of both the Central and State Governments which has afforded little scope about the knowledge of the extent of bio-diversity, of micro-organisms, particularly of bacteria and viruses. Among the North Eastern States, Meghalaya is considered to be a state that has the largest faunal and floral diversity. The State recorded a total of 5538 species of faunal wealth in the country[17].

'Land' and 'Forest' are the two important endowments of nature on humankind. They have both played a singular role in the social, economic and cultural life of human communities through the centuries and one cannot undermine the importance of land and forest both as a resource and as wealth. As a valuable natural resource, land and forest represent the principal forms of property, a symbol of social status and a constant source of economic and political power. Thus, ownership of these two vital resources has often been the symbol of power and prestige in societies around the world.

Land and Its Classification

According to Khasi land tenure system land has been classified as follows for he purpose of its use, occupation and ownership.

I. Ri Raid Land *(Community Land)*

Ri Raid Land is Community Land which is managed and controlled by the concerned community. Every member of the community has the right of use and occupancy of the *Ri Raid* land without payment of land revenue. The community may be a village, a group of villages or an *elaka*. No person has proprietary, heritable or transferable rights over such land. He has only the right of use and occupancy, and such rights revert to the community when the person ceases to occupy or use the land for a period of three years or more. The only way in which a person can inherit land or obtain transferable rights over such land is by making permanent improvements on the land in the form of permanent buildings or cultivation of permanent crops and plant like fruit trees or cultivation. But these rights lapse if he abandons the land over a long period.

Ri Raid land comprises of many sub-classes which can be categorized as forest lands and non-forest lands.

Forest lands are of the following kinds:

1. *Ri 'Law Kyntang, Ri 'Law Niam or Ri 'Law Lyngdoh:* These are forests in Raid Lands set apart for religious purposes, managed and controlled by the Raid or the village or in the case of the *Ri Law Lyngdoh* by the *Lyngdoh* (Priest) of the community.
2. *Ri 'Law Adong, Ri 'Law Sang, Ri 'Law Shnong:* These are village forests reserved by the villagers so that any member could obtain timber or firewood for personal needs or for use as water catchment areas.
3. *Ri 'Law Sumar:* Which belongs to the individual, clan or the village who had first occupied and afforested then and maintains them thereafter.

Non-forest lands include the following types of land:

1. *Ri Shnong (Village Land):* It is a raid land forming part of the village and can be utilised by any member of the village.
2. *Ri Umsnam (Land Acquired Through War):* It is a raid land which an *'elaka'* had won in the older days 'by the sword'.
3. *Ri Ialeh Mukotdama* (Land Acquired Through Litigation) Those lands which have been acquired through litigation by an *elaka*.

4. *Ri Bamlang (Land Given by the Syiem):* Any land when given over to the community by the *Syiem.*

5. *Ri Bam Syiem* (Land Used by the *Syiem*): Any raid land which has been set apart for the exclusive use of the ruling chief and his clan (*kurs*).

6. *Ri Aitimon Sngewbha:* Any land gifted by private landowners to the community for public use.

II. Ri Kynti *(Private Land)*

'*Kynti*' means 'absolute possession'. Therefore *Ri Kynti* lands are private lands which have been acquired by a man or woman individually, or in the case of a woman, inherited from her mother. Such lands must entirely be distinguished from lands of the clan. Colonel Gurdon (1914: 86-88) notes that privately held lands "may be sub-divided into *Ri-Kur* or lands which are property of the clan, *Ri-Kynti*, family or acquired land property". The clan lands, originally when the population was sparse, were owned by families but as the members of the family increased and a clan was formed out of the increasing number of families sprung from a common ancestress, the lands became the property of the clan instead of the family. Such clan lands are properly demarcated by boundary marks.

Like the *Ri Raid* Land, *Ri Kynti* Land comprises many sub-classes:

1. *Ri Kur (Land Belonging to a Clan):* It is a *Ri Kynti* land which has not yet been divided among the different branches of a clan or among different families of a branch of a clan. This land is apportionable by a *dorbar kur* (clan council) or *dorbar kpoh* (council of a branch of the clan) as the case may be.

2. *Ri Nongtymmen (Land Owned by Inheritance):* Is *Ri Kynti* Land which has descended from generation to generation usually after two or three generations. This land is divisible or apportionable by a *dorbar* of the clan or by a branch of the clan if already divided among the several branches thereof. The head of the family, i.e. the mother may also divide this land among her children, usually daughters.

3. *Ri Maw (Stone Land or Land Acquired by Purchase):* Is *Ri Kynti* Land acquired by right of purchase or by right of apportionment

among the member of the family or of the clan and the holders thereof have the right to erect boundary stones to demarcate their respective lots.

4. *Ri Seng:* Is *Ri Kynti* Land acquired from ancient time by a number of different clans or families and has not been divided. Income from this land is divided among the households of the clans or families holding it. The management of *Ri Seng* is in the hands of the representative elected by members of all owing clans or families. In certain cases, such lands may also devolve on male descendants when the clan or families have become extinct, that is when their female relations have died leaving no female issues.

5. *Ri Dakhol* (Land Obtained by Purchase or Right of Occupation): Is land over which a person has obtained *Ri Kynti* rights by right of occupation and mauling permanent improvements thereon or by right of purchase or winning a court case.

6. *Ri Shyieng* (Land Used for Religious Rites by the *Khadduh*): Is a portion of *Ri kur* specially allotted to *Ka Khadduh* (youngest daughter) of a clan or a family to enable her to meet the expenses connected with the performance of religious rites ceremonies concerning the clan, *kpoh* or family, like depositing of the ashes of the dead in the co-urns of the clan. Such land is generally given to *Ka Khadduh* as an additional share.

7. *Ri Lyngdoh:* Is *Ri Kynti* land of the *Lyngdoh* or Priest of a particular native state.

8. *Ri Syiem:* Is *Ri Kynti* land of the *Syiem's* clan. In some *syiemships* it can be Raid Land set apart for maintenance of the *Syiem's* clan.

9. *Ri Iapduh (Land of a Clan that has Become Extinct):* Is *Ri Kynti land* of a clan or a family which has become extinct. Such land according to the time-honoured custom reverts to the chief who is immune from a curse on that family but who will keep it for the *elaka* as *Ri Raid* or as *Ri Bam Syiem* for the family of a ruling chief (Report of the Land Reforms Commission).

Notes

1. Gordon, PRT, *The Khasis*, pp. xxi-xxii.

2. Bareh, Hamlet, *The History and Culture of the Khasi People,* 1985, p.-10.
3. Sen, Soumen. *Social and State Formation in Khasi-Jaintia Hills,* 1985, p. 7.
4. Rymbai, R.T. and others, Report of Land Reforms Commission for Khasi Hills Vol. 1, 1973, p. 34.
5. Bareh. Hamlet, *op. cit.,* p. 9.
6. Gurdon, P.R.T., *The Khasis*, 1914.
7. *Op. cit.* Bareh. Hamlet 1985, p. 13.
8. Rana ——, 1989,
9. *Op. cit.* Bareh, Hamlet, 1985, p. 16.
10. *Ibid.*, p. 18.
11. Government of India, Census Report, 2001.
12. R, Gopalakrishnan, *Meghalaya: Land and People*, p. 2.
13. Bareh. Hamlet, *op. cit.* p. 7.
14. Bareh. Hamlet, *Ibid.*, p. 66.
15. *Shillong Times* (English Daily) dated 7-11-2000.
16. *Apphira* (Khasi Daily) Vol.I.III, No. 83, May 14, 1997.
17. *Apphira* (Khasi Daily) dated 14-5-1997.

2

The Khasi Concept of Forest and Environment

The forest or '*ki khlaw ki btap*' as the Khasis name it, has since time immemorial endured as a revered entity. Looking closely at the value system of the Khasi, one finds that it is centred on the Supreme Being, (*U Blei Nongbuh, Nongthaw*) as well as the transmigration of the soul and religious doctrines, which govern the family and social life.[1] Their relation with God is one of esteemed reverence and fear and they believe that God confidently entrusts and commits to them the basic requirements necessary for their survival and provides all their needs. Thus forest, as a natural resource with its bountiful products is freely accessible to humanity.

For a Khasi, the forest is a well loved home, a game sanctuary and also an abode of worship all rolled into one, around which his social, cultural and religious activities revolve. The Khasis bestow a deep sense of veneration and respect on nature, which has been rightly acclaimed by a famous Khasi writer H.O. Mawrie in the following words:[2]

> "U Khasi u im bad ka mariang, bad ka mariang ka im bad u"

This resounding declaration when translated means, "A Khasi lives with nature and nature lives with him".

This statement bears testimony to the fact that nature with all its bounty shares a harmonious relationship with the Khasis.

While delving deeper into the environmental history of the Khasis, one is struck by the close affinity that exists between the three entities of "God", "Nature" and "Man". This is conclusive evidence to the fact that the Khasis uphold an eco-theandric vision of reality where God, Nature and Man form one single and indivisible entity. The earth is honoured and idolized as "*Meiramew*" which literally means 'mother earth'; *Meiramew*, being combination of land, forest, rivers and streams, the Khasis do not divide these elements as separate entities. While God is present in nature, on the hills, mountains, rivers, lakes, forests, etc. man forms an integral part of this natural environment. Thus, there is an inseparable relationship between God, Man and the objects of Nature. The Khasis sanctify nature and all its elements as gifts from God.

The Eco-theandric vision of nature as a universal feature of the religion of the tribals has been well formulated and used by L.P Vidyarthi to describe the ethnography of the sacred city of Gaya and the religious life of the Maler, a tribal community.[3] .The three concepts—a ' Sacred geography', a set of 'sacred perfomances' and a corps of 'sacred specialists' are collectively conceived, and termed by the Malers as a "Sacred Complex". Thus, one finds a similar expression of the 'wholeness of nature' as an abode of spirits in both the Khasis and the Malers.

Forest: A Sacred Entity

The supernatural connotations of forest have occupied an important place in Khasi literature, Khasi legends and folktales and the life and culture of the people as a whole. This 'sacred ' character of the forest finds expression in the customary practice of preserving sacred groves known as 'khlaw kyntang', which are held with high esteem even today. While the Khasis do not deify nature as God, they believe in the existence of "spirits" that are believed to hover or roam around and inhabit the natural surroundings. These spirits are held with great awe and reverence and a Khasi would spare no pains to appease these spirits, because they are looked upon as powerful influences in nature.

The Khasis divide the realm of spirits into two categories according to their intention towards mankind. The spirits with good intention are regarded as godlings or "*Lei*". Each of these godlings presides over a specific function. These deities are supposed to be associated with functions as state welfare, wealth, water, village, etc. The spirits with bad intention are referred to as '*suid*' and are responsible for causing harm and injury, sickness or even death. The Khasis believe that the good spirits protect them only as long as they obey God's commands, but the moment they cease to obey, the evil forces will interfere with their lives in many ways and harm them. Thus, they would speak of a number of spirits associated with objects of nature such as:

- Mountain or hill spirits (*Lei Lum*)
- River spirits (*Lei Wah*)
- Forest spirits (*Lei Khlaw*)
- God of the state (*Lei Mulluk*)
- Water spirits (*Lei Umtong*).

The forest is considered as an abode of the '*Lei*' or good spirits where the '*rngai*' or shadow of the deceased roams about. Therefore, while wandering through the woods, mountains and valleys, it is customary for a Khasi to do so with respect and develop a feeling of reverence towards the natural surroundings.

Forest Wisdom of the Khasis

The ecological wisdom of the Khasis is a wisdom that is solidly based on "experience" and they depend on this knowledge to fulfil most of their day-to-day needs (their economy). Through agriculture, hunting, fishing and gathering a huge range of forest foods and materials with which they make most of their articles of daily use, from houses to ploughs, baskets to leaf-plates. They possess an ancient lore of herbal medicine as well as knowledge about many aspects of nature and human life. Much of this ancient wisdom is today the result of oral tradition. Forest wisdom has enabled the Khasis to live in harmony with nature besides elevating them to such a high pedestal that no animal or living creature could compete with. The following examples throw light on the use of such forest knowledge in understanding what happens in the natural surroundings:

1. The Khasis believe that the flowering of bamboo is a sign that famine is close at hand because it would attract rats that would then be detrimental to farming and cultivation.
2. The pine tree for a Khasi is a symbol of goodwill, nobleness and self-sacrifice because it provides fuel, timber, leaves, etc.
3. When tender leaves start growing on rubber trees, it is indicative that fishes are multiplying in rivers and seas.
4. When the petals of a particular flower called '*kymbat samthiah*' close, the sun begins to set and when the petals open, the sun rises.
5. The flowering of a particular plant called '*tiew diengsong*' is associated with the onset of fever.

Thus, there are lessons to be learnt from the signs of nature. Much of the forest knowledge of the Khasis has been lost today due to the advancement of science and the diminishing role of oral tradition. However, the Khasis still uphold their natural wisdom, which helps them in unveiling the mysteries of life. The Khasis are a community who live in close commune with nature. The strong bond that exists between the Khasi and the environment leads one to believe that the forest, which is a vital component of the environment, is the centre of Khasi socio-economic and cultural life. The Khasis do not consider these elements of the earth and mother as separate entities.

Forests as Sacred Abodes

Preservation of forests as sacred groves has been existent since time immemorial amongst the Khasis. People are mostly governed by their belief systems in conserving these forests. The existence of "*U Ryngkew U Basa*" or "the guardian sprit" in these forests is a belief that has existed amongst the Khasis since time immemorial. The 'guardian spirit', according to them, resides in the forest and takes care of the village community and protects them from sickness, pain, invasion by enemies, etc. Therefore, destroying or cutting of trees, grass, etc. from these groves is considered to be against the wish of *U Ryngkew U Basa* and, therefore, people are afraid of these spirits.

"*Law Kyntang*" as they are generally known are also known by various names such as "*Law Lyngdoh*" or "*Law Niam*". These forests are set aside for religious purposes and are managed by the Lyngdoh (a religious priest) or any other person to whom the religious ceremonies for the particular locality are entrusted. Till today, these sacred groves are held in high esteem and every now and then religious ceremonies including worship of forest deities, dances and rituals are regularly performed, by the '*Lyngdoh*' together with the villagers inside the grove. Mention may be made of the sacred grove at Pahampdem village located at Ri Bhoi district which is popularly known by the local people as '*U Lum Mawker*' or '*U Lum Umphar*'. The grove is the biggest recorded sacred grove in the state with an area of 900 ha.

This grove belongs to the '*Lyngdoh Syntiew*' clan and so management of the grove is left to the clan council. Besides its religious significance, these groves serve as a natural habitat for many rare species of flora and fauna. The importance of sacred groves in biodiversity conservation has also been recognised in recent times. In Meghalaya, sacred groves belong either to private owners or to clans and communities. As such, the legal status accorded to these groves is in accordance with the acts of the respective District Councils of Khasi, Jaintia and Garo Hills.

The United Khasi-Jaintia Hills Autonomous District (Management and Control of Forests) Act 1958, also referred to as Act 1 of 1958 is the principal act for the management and control of the forests in the autonomous district area . This act was later appended with the United Khasi-Jaintia Hills Autonomous District rules or Rules 1960. According to the Rules 1960, all the private forests including sacred groves (*Law Lyngdoh, Law Kyntang* and *Law Niam*) in the area of the District Council are to be registered with the Chief Forest Officer mentioning the home addresses of with the boundaries and such other particulars of the forests as may be required. No timber or forest produce from *Law Kyntang*, *Law Lyngdoh* and *Law Niam* are allowed to be felled or removed except for purposes in connection with religious functions or ceremonies recognised and sanctioned by the *Lyngdoh* (religious head) and other persons in accordance with Section 4(b) (Section 9 of the Act 1958).

Table 2.1: Locations and Estimated Area of Sacred Forests in East Khasi Hills, West Khasi Hills, Ri Bhoi, Jaintia Hills, West Garo Hills and East Garo Hills Districts of Meghalaya

Sl. No.	*Names of the Groves*	*Distance from Shillong (km)*	*Area (ha)*	*Village*	*Controlling Authority (Syiemship/ Dolloiship/ Nokmaship etc.)*
JAINTIA HILLS					
1.	Blai Law	85	0.01	Raliang	Raliang Dolloiship
2.	Poh Puja Ko Patti	74	4		Raliang Dolloiship
3.	Poh Moorang	90	20	Raliang	Raliang Dolloiship
4.	Ka Pun Lyngdoh	85	15	Raliang	Raliang Dolloiship
5.	Khlaw Byrsan	80	50	Raliang	Raliang Dolloiship
6.	Poh Lyngdoh	74	30	Shangpung	Shangpung Dolloiship
7.	Law Kyntang	74	400	Shangpung	Shangpung Dolloiship
8.	Khlaw Blai	105	15	Dien Shynrum	Rymbai Dolloiship
9.	Khloo Paiu Ram Pyrthai	60	150	Panaliar	Jowai Dolloiship
10.	Trepale Jowai	60	70	Panaliar	Jowai Dolloiship
11.	Khloo Lyngdoh	60	15	Panaliar	Jowai Dolloiship
12.	Mokhain Sacred Grove	60	45	Khimmusiang	Jowai Dolloiship
13.	Dpepat Myndihati	110	15	Myndihati	Sutnga Dolloiship
14.	Lumtiniang Mokaiaw Syndai	115	25	Syndai	Satpator Dolloiship
RI BHOI					
16.	Pahampdem	55	900	Paham-pdem	Raid Umsaw-Nongkharai
17.	Nonglyngdoh	55	90	Nongkhrah	Nongpoh Sirdarship
18.	Sohpetbneng Sacred Grove	40	90	Nongkhrah	Nongpoh Sirdarship
EAST KHASI HILLS					
19.	Law Lyngdoh	25	75	Mawphlang	Mawphlang Lyndohship
20.	Law Lyngdoh Nongkrem	14	6	Smit	Khyrim Syiemship
21.	Lum Shillong	8	7	Laitkor	Khyrim Syiemship
22.	Law Kyntang	53	50	Khlieh Shnong	Sohra Syiemship
23.	Law Adong	53	90	Khlieh Shnong	Sohra Syiemship
24.	Khlaw Ram Jadong	55	50	Mawsmai	Mawsmai Syiemship
25.	Law Blei Bah	55	120	Mawsmai	Mawsmai Syiemship
26.	Mawlong Syiem	55	120	Mawsmai	Mawsmai Syiemship
27.	Pom Shandi	55	80	Mawsmai	Mawsmai Syiemship
28.	Law Adong	55	400	Mawsmai	Mawsmai Syiemship
29.	Law Suidnoh	45	80	Laitryngew	Sohra Syiemship
30.	Law-u-Niang	45	10	Laitryngew	Sohra Syiemship

(Contd.)

Table 2.1 (*Contd.*)

Sl. No.	*Names of the Groves*	*Distance from Shillong (km)*	*Area (ha)*	*Village*	*Controlling Authority (Syiemship/ Dolloiship/ Nokmaship etc.)*
31.	Madan Jadu	45	5	Laitryngew	Sohra Syiemship
32.	Law-ar-Liang	38	25	Khadar Blang	Khyrim Syiemship
33.	Lum Diengjri	75	25	Khadar Shnong	Sohra Syiemship
34.	Mawmang Sacred Grove	60	15	Khadar Shnong	Sohra Syiemship
35.	Wahkhen Sacred Grove	35	10	Khadar Blang	Khyrim Syiemship
36.	Law Lieng	42	20	Sohra Rim	Khatsawphra Syiemship
37.	Law Mawsaptur	42	50	Sohra Rim	Sohra Syiemship
38.	Law Dymmiew	42	200	Sohra Rim	Sohra Syiemship
39.	Law Nongshim	43	5	Mawmih	Sohra Syiemship
40.	Mawsawa	55	50	Mawmluh	Sohra Syiemship
41.	Mawryot	62	40	Wahlong	Wahlong Sirdarship
42.	Niangdoh	62	30	Wahlong	Wahlong Sirdarship
43.	Rijaw	62	35	Wahlong	Wahlong Sirdarship
44.	Umtong	63	400	Umwai	Umwai Sirdarship
45.	Diengkain	63	400	Umwai	Umwai Sirdarship
46.	Mawthong	63	600	Umwai	Umwai Sirdarship
47.	Maw Kyrngah	63	1200	Umwai	Umwai Sirdarship
48.	Kynsang	65	150	Mawlong	Mawlong Sirdarship
49.	Umthri	65	80	Mawlong	Mawlong Sirdarship
50.	Umkatait	65	100	Mawlong	Mawlong Sirdarship
51.	Ulaw Lyngdoh	91	90	Nong-lyngkien	Maharam Syiemship
52.	Ulum Sanglia	92	45	Nong-lyngkien	Maharam Syiemship
53.	Ulaw Blei	90	55	Nong-lyngkien	Maharam Syiemship
54.	Law Lyngdoh	80	200	Nonglang	Maharam Syiemship
55.	Law Kyntang	80	300	Mawlang-wiar	Maharam Syiemship
56.	Law Kyntang	75	100	Mawten	Maharam Syiemship
57.	Law Lyngdoh	70	400	Rangmaw	Maharam Syiemship
58.	Law Kyntang	90	100	Mawthawiaw	Maharam Syiemship

(*Contd.*)

Table 2.1 (*Contd.*)

Sl. No.	Names of the Groves	Distance from Shillong (km)	Area (ha)	Village	Controlling Authority (Syiemship/ Dolloiship/ Nokmaship etc.)
59.	Nongsynrih Sacred Grove	92	100	Nongsynrih	Maharam Syiemship
60.	Law Lyngdoh	75	50	Nonglait	Maharam Syiemship
61.	Law Adong Lyngdoh Mawlong	43	200	Mawlong	Nongkhlaw Syiemship
62.	Kyllai Lyngngum	104	80	Marian	Nobosohphoh Syiemship
63.	Lyngdoh Mawnai Sacred Grove	104	80	Mawnai	Nobosohphoh Syiemship

Forest in Khasi Rituals and Ceremonies

Rituals abound in Khasi religion and culture. In the words of H.O. Mawrie, *"Ka Kolshor bad ka niam ki long kiba la ngam ha ki thied snam jong ngi kum ka jaitbynriew bad ban bret ia ki ka long kumba patar da lade ia lade."* ("Rituals are a part and parcel of our culture. They have embedded their roots deep down in our flesh and blood and to think of mankind to throw away either of them is to tear oneself apart.") There are rituals pertaining to three important stages in one's life:

(1) Naming ceremony (*ka jer ka thoh*)
(2) Marriage (*poikha-poiman*)
(3) Death (*niam ïap*)

Naming Ceremony

The following are some instances of the use of forest products during the birth ceremony:

(a) When the child is born, a sharp splinter of bamboo cuts the umbilical cord. No knife can be used on this occasion.

(b) When the umbilical cord, after being tied falls off, a ritual is performed by offering worship to certain water deities '*Ka blei sam-um*' and also to forest spirit '*U 'suid bri*' or "*U 'suid khlaw*'.
(c) For the naming ceremony, the pounded rice flour is placed on a bamboo winnower called '*U prah.*'
(d) A plantain leaf is used to place five pieces of '*Kha piah*' or dried fish.
(e) Liquor is placed in a gourd (*klong*).

Marriage Ceremony

A simple wedding ceremony of the Khasi would include the exchange of distilled liquor from two gourds (*klong*) which are mixed together. The priest then says a prayer of blessing over the couple and pours the entire liquor on to the three '*khapiah*' or dry fish. These are then placed in a container and preserved over the hearth.

Death Ceremony

The following instances of the use of forest products are evident in death ceremonies of the Khasis:

(a) The dead body is laid on a mat (*japung*) made of bamboo.
(b) A small bamboo basket (*ka shang*) is hung up over the head of the corpse.
(c) Sometimes the body is placed in a coffin, which is laid on a bamboo bier (*ka krong*).
(d) As the funeral party sets out to the bone repository (*mawshieng*), one person in front strews a line of route leaves of the tree known by the Khasis as '*dieng shit*'. If any stream is to be crossed, a rough bridge is made of branches and grass. This trail of leaves and the bridges are intended to guide the spirit of the deceased to the cairn.

Forest Legends and Folklore

Forest myths and legends have played an important role in enriching the ecological history of societies around the world. Similarly, folklore is the hallmark of people's ethical and aesthetic norms and their values of life and is the index of the social, cultural and emotional evolution of that society. Folklore represents the archaic thought of mankind, their sense of Human values and their worldview. It is a mirror through which one can perceive the past cultural and historical landscape of a people. Dr. Suniti Kumar Chatterjee called folklore "*Lokayana*" that signifies a way of life of a community (*Loka* - community, *yana* - way of life).

The Khasis have maintained a close symbiotic relationship with environment since time immemorial and their ethno-cultural traits have been greatly influenced by the natural surroundings. A well-known Khasi legend centres on the belief in "*U Diengiei*", a giant tree that is very popular among them. According to this legend there was a very tall and gigantic tree at Lum Diengiei with its branches spread far and wide that covered the sun overshadowing the earth. The whole world became dark and damp and the people, deprived of the warmth of the sun and light suffered from ill-health, disease and death. So they held their village council meetings and decided to cut down the tree, and ultimately it was only after they had felled the tree that they could enjoy health, peace and happiness. This folktale throws ample light on the attitude and perception of the ancient Khasis towards tree and forest. They considered forest as the home of Gods and evil spirits, as something dreadful and looked them with a sense of awe and reverence.

The Khasi folklore and legends, "*Khanatang bad Puriskam*" are mostly woven around the various forces of nature such as the hills and vales, rocks and caves, the flora and fauna. These elements of nature are personified in the legends as the mother and son, husband and wife and friend and foe according to their natural behaviours, their love, hate, jealousy, pride and vanity which are projected out before the listeners with the sole purpose of teaching moral and spiritual values. To give a few examples out of many, in the folktale of "*U Klew bad ka Sngi*" (The Peacock and the Sun), the peacock has been personified as the husband of the sun. Both of them lived happily in the sky. One fine morning the peacock saw a beautiful mustard field in full bloom on earth below.

He thought that it was the most beautiful maiden he had ever seen. Thereupon, he decided to fly down to earth and meet her. The sun, his wife, begged him not to go leaving her behind, but that did not deter him. But on descending on the earth he could see that the beautiful virgin was nothing but a mere field of mustard plants. The peacock lamented for his silly mistake and shed his tears all upon his feathers, which created those spots that the peacock still carries on his wings. This story gives the moral lesson of conjugal fidelity between husband and wife.

Another famous legend is about the use of betel nut, betel leaf and tobacco, which is an essential item among the Khasi. The story is about a poor couple "U Shing" and his wife "Ka Lak" who had a very intimate well to do friend by the name of "U Nik Mahajon". Whenever, the couple visited their friend's house, they were welcomed with respect and were treated to sumptuous meals. However, one day when U Nik Mahajon visited the couple, they were taken by surprise not to find anything in the house to offer to their guest. "Ka Lak" went round the neighbourhood begging for some food but came back empty handed. Overcome by shame and desperation, the couple took a knife and killed themselves. When U Nik Mahajon found them dead in the kitchen and understood the cause for the suicide, he too took the same knife and ended his life in the same manner.

It so happened that a thief entered the house that night and seeing the three dead bodies, understood that he would be blamed for this so in utter desperation, he too ended his own life. When the people realized this sad event, they begged God to give them a simpler way of welcoming friends. The ancient Khasis have compared these three people to the three most valued things in the household, namely, the betel nut, leaf and lime, and tobacco. The betel nut stands for the rich friend, the betel leaf and the lime to the couple and the tobacco to the thief. This legend accounts for the Khasi way of greeting a guest no matter how poor or rich they may be, it has been a norm of hospitality to offer *kwai* (betel nut, leaf and lime) to welcome friends and guests into their homes.

Forests are a treasure trove of a large variety of food. It is estimated that 60-70 per cent of food consumed by the tribals comes from the forest. It is a familiar sight to see Khasi women and children setting off into the woods to collect edible fruits and roots. They look upon the forest as the ultimate storehouse of wealth, a source of immediate help at difficult times, a readymade kitchen store-house and a Khasi would spare no chance to run to the forest and grab any edible delicacy to offer to an unexpected guest who just pays a sudden visit.

Forest produces such as tubers, rhizome, succulent shoots, fruits and mushrooms have provided the villagers with an alternative source of economic activity besides supplementing their basic requirements of food. An estimated study reveals that most of the village folk who still continue the collection of wild mushroom from the Upper Shillong Reserve Forest in Laitkor peak collects about 5 kgs. of mushroom and wild fruits per day per head and sell them in the markets. Many Khasi families in Bhoi Area district of Khasi Hills live by collecting and selling bamboo-shoots and other wild vegetables seasonally. An interesting study made by a well known Khasi author, S. Khongsit brings out a list of 113 wild food items comprising of edible leaves, roots, bark of trees, fruits and vegetables that are procured from the forest which begin their names with the prefix "*Ja*", meaning 'cooked rice' in Khasi language. This fact affords us ample evidence to prove that the Khasis traditionally substitute cooked rice by these edible forest produces as their daily diet.

With the increasing realization of medicinal values of plants and herbs found in the forests, trading in medicinal plants has become a hidden economy for many Khasi villagers. According to a research conducted by the North Eastern Bio-diversity Research Cell Shillong, the North Eastern Region alone has more than 10,278 plant species that constitute more than 17 per cent of the country's genetic resources. A preliminary survey conducted on the use of medicinal plants reveal that there were over 200 Khasi herbal practitioners who use medicinal plants and herbs for treatment in East Khasi Hills, West Khasi Hills, Jaintia Hills and Ri Bhoi districts. There is a growing concern among the local herbal practitioners and environmentally conscious citizens for the rapid depletion of valuable herbs and plants due to illegal smuggling and wanton destruction of forests and the absence of effective law enforcement agency in these areas. A lurking danger of biopiracy, which could lead to unrestricted depletion of the State's natural bio-resources is clearly evident. In order to protect and develop the unique Khasi folklore of indigenous medicine (*Dawai kynbat*) and to save the store of valuable medicinal plants and herbs from extinction there is an urgent need to integrate the Khasi system of treatment with modern health care system of the state and to intensify vigilance against pilfering of important species of medicinal plants from their pristine habitats.

Like many other hill people of the North East, the economy of the Khasi is essentially land and forest oriented. Agriculture is the mainstay of the people, which is largely carried out, in primitive method called *jhum* or shifting cultivation. This practice is however considered destructive as vast areas of forest is butchered and burnt down every year to raise multiple crops for the livelihood of the people. Those lands are used again for jhum cultivation after a gap of three to five years repeating the same process of cutting and burning forests without allowing reasonable time to forest to rejuvenate. In Khasi Hills Jhum cultivation, which is locally known as "*thang shyrti*" is still practiced by a large number of households although the number of jhumias has appreciably come down.

Nature has endowed the Khasi homeland with the kind of soil and climate suitable for a wide variety of crops, fruits and vegetables. The Central plateau of the district is suitable for growing high altitude paddy, maize, millets, potato and temperate fruits and vegetables; while the southern slopes bordering Bangladesh grows plantation crops like oranges, bananas, pineapples, ereca-nuts, betel leaves, bay leaf, etc. In the northern side of the district bordering Assam, paddy, maize, banana, and pineapple are widely grown. But the Khasi economy has essentially remained a tribal economy till today, characterized by simple technology and primitive method due to geographical isolation, hilly terrain and single-family system of production and consumption. No appreciable change appears to have taken place in the style and technique of rural economy despite Government efforts, during the last fifty years, for improved agricultural practice and diversified economy.

A majority of the village industries in the Khasi Hills are forest based. Industries like carpentry, cane and bamboo work, bee-keeping, broomstick making, etc. derive their raw materials from the forest which provides employment opportunities to a large section of the rural people who work in the forests by felling trees and sawing timbers in lime kilns and burning and selling charcoal. The womenfolk and children of the poor families traditionally eke out their living by cutting and selling firewood, collecting broomstick, selling wild fruits and vegetables while the men folk penetrate deeper into the forest and gather valuable orchids and wild flora for earning handsome prices for the urban rich.

Thus forest, which constitutes an integral component of the environment, occupies the central place in the social and religious life of the Khasi. The forest has always been a ubiquitous item in all activities of man and it will continue to remain so with added interest and opportunties. It is on the forest resource that ultimately their future economy can find sound footing (Mathew, 1980:26).

Jhum Cultivation

Shifting cultivation commonly known as "*jhumming*" is one of the most ancient systems of farming believed to have originated in the Neolithic period around 7000 BC. It is called slash and burn method of cultivation. The system is regarded as the first step in transition from food gathering and hunting to crop husbandry. It is still practised in the hill areas of the North East states and in certain pockets of the country. Among the Khasis, this system of cultivation is known as "*Thang shyrti*" or "*Thang bun*". Essential features of *jhum* cultivation with special reference to Khasi Hills is as follows:

1. *Site selection*: Selection of sites for *jhum* practices is usually done by the individual owners of the land according to the needs of the family and family size. This is usually done before the month of December.
2. *Jungle cutting*: This operation is usually done in the months of December to January.
3. *Drying of Debris*: This operation follows just after the jungle is cleared and the debris is left to dry in the open.
4. *Burning*: Setting of fire to the dried debris is done from mid February to March. This operation is done with care so as to avoid forest fires from spreading across to other hills, which were not meant for '*jhumming*'.
5. *Sowing/Planting*: Sowing and planting of various crops is done in an intimate mixture by dibbling with a pointed staff of wood. Upland paddy is the main crop grown in mixture with maize, millet, sorghum, tapioca, chillies, cotton, turmeric, pumpkin, etc.

6. *The hutments* of the village now remain at the same place in contrast to earlier days when the whole village shifted to new site.
7. *Cropping is done with minimum tillage*: No animals or large implements are used by the *jhum* cultivators for preparing land. The only implements used are the chopping knife, sickle, dibbling stick, spade and hoe.
8. There is practically no capital investment except labour and the seeds, which usually come from the household.

Jhum cultivation has a chain of effects and after-effects leading to multifarious adverse conditions. The following chart shows, at a glance, how the system causes far-reaching disturbances in the conditions of the soil leading to changes in the climate, ecological imbalance and the environmental degradation, besides the immediate results of fertility loss and low productivity of crops.

Firstly, the process of cutting and burning, *jhum* causes denudation of forests leading to two consequences, viz. ecological imbalance and elimination of the sources of water. Secondly, it causes soil erosion leading to silting up of rivers and streams which causes flood, on the other hand it affects fertility of the soil resulting in low productivity and pressure on land. Thirdly, the system of *jhum* is a primitive method with low technology involving much labour without subsidiary income. Lastly, it is a socially degrading system, detrimental to development programme and conservative in spirit and attitude of the *jhumias*.

Forest for Medicine

The Khasis are known for their unique knowledge about plants wealth and herbals drugs in curing diseases. The origin of Khasi system of medicine is not known, as Khasi folklore and legend are silent about its origin. But the psychological, social and cultural contribution to this system is very prominent.

Since time immemorial the folk medicine has been evolved, practised and developed and even today it has an enormous resource potential for the care and management of health problems. The traditional system of medicine of the Khasis, unlike that of other communities of India, is not looked down upon as primitive and crude way of treatment, but majority of the rural population in Khasi Hills still rely on this for their primary health care needs. In this case one cannot deny that the socio-cultural and psychological forces play a large part in determining the causes, nature and means of counteracting illness. Most of the diseases and social disabilities arise from the social conditions, unhealthy lifestyle, food-habits and high-risk behaviour of the community. The prevalence of endemic and racial diseases is the example of this. Mr. William C. Cockerham writes – "Health is, therefore, not simply a matter of biology but involves a number of factors that are social, cultural, political and economic in nature".

Nearly 400 B.C. ago, Hippocrates, the Greek Physician, pointed out that human well-being is influenced by the totality of environmental factors, living habits or lifestyle, climate, topography of the land and the quality of air, water and food.

It is for this reason that forest plays a great role in determining the problems and management of health of a community. The Khasi Hills are abounding in large varieties of medicinal plants and herbs.

Its climate, rainfall, soil condition and topography contribute to the growth of dark forests, shrubs and thickets, which are the ideal home to valuable medicinal plants. Many of these plants, which are often considered as weeds, are very important for their medicinal properties.

Table 2.2 shows the major plants and herbs available in Khasi hills and the diseases treated by those plants.

Table 2.2 : Major Plants and Herbs in Khasi Hills

Sl. No.	*Scientific Name*	*Local Name*	*Parts Used*	*Diseases Treated*
1.	Andrographis paniculata	Kynbat jyrngam	Roots	Rheumatic pains, Anti-helmintic
2.	Ageratum conyzoides	Kynbat blumyngai	Leaves	Cuts, Bleeding, Antidote for snakebite.
3.	Artemisia nilagirica	Khel bijak	Leaves	Asthma, Brain diseases, Sores.
4	Centela asiatica	Kynbat Moina/ Khleiñ Syiar	Leaves & roots	Dysentery, Blood pressure, Skin diseases

(Contd.)

Table 2.2 (*Contd.*)

Sl. No.	Scientific Name	Local Name	Parts Used	Diseases Treated
5.	Flemingia vestita	Sohphlang	Root bank	Tape worms and worms eradication
6.	Mimosa pudica	Kynbat samthiah	Leaves, roots & stems	Piles, Hydrocele, Scorpion sting.
7.	Eupatorium odoratum	Krah-lynroh	Leaf	Bleeding and Dysentery.
8.	Galinsoga parviflora	Tiew-lien	Leaves	Bleeding and Insect sting.
9.	Drymaria cordata	Thei phelwang	Whole plant	Diarrhoea, Vomiting, Urinary problem, antidote for snakebite.
10.	Imaptiens racemosa		Leaves & roots	Rheumatic pains.
11.	Nepethes khasiana	Tiew rakot	Pitcher	Ear disease and cholera.
12.	Oxalis corniculata	Soh-dkhiew	Leaves	Cough, snakebite, dysentery.
13.	Potentila fulgens	Lyngniang-bru	Whole plant	Colic pain, spasmodic trouble, pyorrhoea.
14.	Plantago major	Shkor Blang	Leaves & roots	Bleeding injuries/wounds
15.	Panax pseudoginseng	Kynbat syieng jinseng	Roots	Aphrodisiac, Hypothermia, Asthma, Rheumatism.
16.	Solanum xanthocarpum	Dieng-phydok bakthang	Roots & fruits	Flatulence, Threadworm, Tuberculosis.
17.	Taxus bacata	Sohblei	Leaves	Aphrodisiac, Epilepsy & Irregular menstruation.
18.	Viscum articulatum	Mangkariang khlem sla	Whole plant	Snakebite, wounds.
19.	Zinger officinalis	Sying	Rhizoma	Cough, Rheumatism.
20.	Mikania micrantha	Momoshathap	Leaves	Stomach trouble.
21.	Polygonum orientale	Agasom	Leaves	Severe headache.
22.	Uraria crinita	Dieng kharia	Roots	High fevers.
23.	Chenopodium ambroisioides	Slah sam	Plant	Nervous tension.
24.	Emilia sonchifolia	Soh Byshet	*Leaf juice*	Eye problems.
25.	Musa sapientum	Ka Kait	*Root, fruit, stem*	Dysentery, Diarrhoea, Boil, Worms.

Notes

1. Bareh, Hamlet, *The History and Culture of the Khasi People*, 2001.
2. Mawrie, *H.o, Ka Pyrkhat U Khasi*, 1972.
3. Vidyarthi, L.P., *The Maler: The Nature-Man-Spirit-Complex in a Hill Tribe*, 1963, p-140.

3

A Brief History of Colonial Forestry in Khasi and Jaintia Hills

Geographically India is a tremendous diversity—from the bare snowy mountains in the north to the tropical rain forests in the south, from the arid desert in the west to the alluvial flood ridden plains in the east, India represents a bewildering picture of diverse natural setting with multi-racial, cultural, linguistic and religious demography. The culture of India has exhibited diverse mode of resource control corresponding to different agro-climatic and vegetative zones.

Forests have been the traditional abode of men especially in India where the *rishis* and *acharyas*, the hermits and monks have evolved a forest culture by living in *ashramas* deep in the heart of nature among the high Himalayas. To the ancient Indians, therefore, forest represented the sacred home—*arannyany* where the seers and sages performed rigorous *Tapasyas* (ordeal-some meditation) for achieving coveted blessings from god. It is from such a revered tradition that the genesis of the forest history of India began, passed through various phases of human development and culture until it passed under the British colonial rule. The mode of ancient culture and usages of forest drastically changed and the very concept of Indian forest as—"*Arannyani*" vanished into the thin air. Man's past outlook towards forest as one like the "Garden of Eden,—full of trees and pleasing to the eye and good for food"(Genesis 2:9), changed to that of store-house of natural resources ready for human exploitation. Man's greed for material gratification led him to indulge in ruthless assault on the pristine beauty and bounty of nature. The awareness of men's dependence upon nature had a long ancestry; but role of men as the 'maker and unmaker' of nature came as a new realisation gained only after the British rule in India.[1] Thus the British government, after taking over possession of India, assumed the new role in dealing with the forest resources of the country in a manner best suited to their purpose.

The following paragraphs discuss, at some length, the history of British policy and administration on forest in Assam and its impact on the socio-economic condition of the people.

Colonial Forestry in Assam

Assam, the country of Ahoms, which was under frequent invasions of the Burmese, and an object of internal feuds and intrigues, became a part of British Empire on February 24th, 1826 after the Treaty of Yandaboo. In a quick succession the Khasi Hills, an amalgam of numerous small independent Khasi states and the Jaintia Hills, ancient kingdom of Jaintias, also passed into the hands of the British and became a part of the province of Assam. Since that time till the end of colonial rule Khasi and Jaintia Hills remained within Assam as one of its districts. The Khasi and Jaintia Hills district was declared as Partially Excluded Areas for the purpose of all administration. The Government of India (Excluded and Partially Areas) Order 1936 declared the Naga Hills district, Lushai Hills district, the North Cachar Sub-division of the Cachar district and the Frontier tracts as Excluded Areas. The Garo Hills district, Khasi and Jaintia Hills district (excluding Shillong) and the Mikir Hills district were declared as Partially Excluded Areas.[2] Therefore, while discussing about the history of colonial forestry of Khasi and Jaintia Hills, it will be pertinent, to deal with the forestry of composite Assam first, and thereafter with Khasi and Jaintia Hills district separately.

Physiography and Environment of Assam

Assam lies at the foot of the Eastern Himalayas with the highest altitude of 7,756 metres in the north-east. Its physiography is dominated by the mighty Brahmaputra river which flows from east to the west cutting across the state into two halves. The river Brahmaputra is also known for its frequent floods in the state causing extensive damage to crops and untold miseries to people. Both the banks of the river constitute vast plain lands called the Brahmaputra valleys and are characterised by fertile alluvial soil with hot tropical climate. On the far south of Assam lie hilly regions with moderate and high hills reaching up to 6000 ft. above sea level where tribal people with distinct languages and cultures, such as—Khasi and Jaintias, Garos, Nagas, Mizos, Mikirs live. The rainfall in this region is one of the highest in the world which keeps the soil moisture and fertile contributing to thick and luxuriant growth of trees, shrubs and grass in their abundance and great variety.

The forests of Assam are home to diverse species of birds and animals which attract the interest of tourists. The one horned rhinoceros is one of the unique possession of the state, the horn of which is considered to be a precious object. In ancient times, Assam was known more for her elephants which were widely used in fighting wars and hunting expeditions by kings and the nobles. They were also habitually put into hard work for carrying heavy objects. During medieval times the elephants in Assam were in high demand by the Mughals and the Indian native kings who wanted to use them in battles.

Assam, described variously as the land of blue hills and green forests, is one of the hotspots of bio-diversity. It is a home to great variety of flora and fauna some of which are rare. The vast wealth of natural forest grown in humid tropical and sub-tropical forests characterised by their endemic nature have always fascinated botanists, ecologists, geneticists and students of environment.[3] In the northern region of the river Brahmaputra sal trees (Shorea robusts) grow extensively and also vast stretches of grassland were seen often without a tree for miles.[4] Further to the north, along the foot of Himalayas bordering Bhutan, evergreen forests grow extensively stretching down to the districts of Goalpara and Darrang. To the South of Brahmaputra, in the plain belts of Naga Hills, Mikir Hills and Garo Hills Teak, sal, sissu and many other valuable species of hardwood trees are found. Further to the south, the hilly regions of Khasi and Jaintia Hills and Garo Hills are clad with luxuriant evergreen forests of Pine (*Pinus khasya*) variety and occur thick bamboo groves mixed with grass, fruit and wild banana trees all along the hill slopes and deep gorges.

Early British Rule

Medieval Assam did not experience large scale deforestation as it happened in the later period. Before, the advent of the British the vast natural wealth of forests that grew wild in the jungles were hardly used by the people of Assam except for meagre home consumption that accounted extremely negligible. They used forest products primarily for building houses, making boats and agricultural appliances and for firewood, etc. The valuable trees, bamboos, grass and other minor produces were left to grow there, in thick and dense. The Mughals were marginally interested in trading primarily with aromatic trees like *aloes wood* (the heart of Aquilaria agallocha, which contains a resinous substance).[5] The British were, however, attracted by the vast natural wealth lying waste in the form of valuable forest products hitherto unused by the inhabitants of Assam. They quickly realised the utility and commercial value of timber that could be prospected from the wild and virgin forests of Assam. The forests contained certain species of hard and durable qualities of wood in abundance which were in high demand in England for ship building. During 1860s Great Britain emerged as the world's number one country in exploiting and denuding its own forests to meet the requirement of timber for ship-building and iron-smelting.[6] Such being the demand for timber in England during the advent of the British in Assam the colonial government promptly decided to start its control and management over the precious natural resource of Assam. The British urgently felt the necessity of a well defined forest policy in order to preserve, protect and harness the rich benefit from the vast forest resources. Besides the direct benefits derived from forest products, the role of green vegetations in protecting top soil from being eroded did not escape the notice of the botanists. B. Ribbentrop, the Inspector General of Forests to the Government of India observed—"Inundation and carrying away of top soil by torrents because of destruction of forests have also been observed in Assam, where the surface soil in many tea-gardens has been washed away and where the yield has dwindled down to next to nothing"[7] As in other provinces of India, the necessity of a well organised forest administration in Assam was keenly observed by the government. With this end in view in 1868, a Forest Department was established, for the first time, in Assam, under the Bengal Rules 1865 and placed under an Assistant Conservator of Forest.[8]

For the purpose of smooth and efficient administration of forests in the province the British divided it into two divisions in 1874, each headed by an Assistant Conservator of Forests with a Deputy Conservator having overall charge of the entire province. The Upper Assam Division comprised the former district of Lakhimpur, Sibsagar and the Naga Hills, while the Lower Assam Division included Kamrup, Nowgong, Darrang and Khasi and Jaintia Hills.[9] Assam forest was classified into two broad divisions—Reserved forest and Open forest. The reserved forests were the property of the government while the open forests were allowed to be used by public provided that certain reserved trees as were notified and marked upon from time to time by Forest Department were not removed or felled. The forest administration of Assam was conducted in accordance with Forest Act 1865 which was already in force in other parts of India. This Act of 1865 was followed by Act VII of 1869 in order to make applicable certain rules relating to forest administration in Burma which did not find mention in the original Act of 1865. It has often been mentioned, that the strength of colonial forestry primarily lay in its political superiority and availability of technologies of resource use, which were new to India. But what is well recognized was the fact that the major imperative of colonial forestry was basically dictated by the commercial utility of timber rather than the broader social or environmental considerations.

During the first few decades of its rule, the colonial policy in India was characterized by a total indifference towards the needs of forest conservancy. The forest was not considered as a very important object to protect and preserve. Agriculture was given more priority than anything else and large scale forest lands were settled to cultivators for growing crops. It was often argued—"Cultivation must extend and its interests are not to be forgotten".[10] In fact, it was not until the middle of the nineteenth century, that the Raj witnessed a "fierce onslaught" on India's forest.[11] The idea of protecting the forest of Assam and taking care and management occurred to the government, for the first time in 1850 when the wood cutters from Bengal had been felling Assam sal trees indiscriminately from Goalpara district. As a measure to control this activity the government introduced a tax system to be paid at the rate of Rs. 15 per hundred logs from which the revenue accrued to government was estimated at Rs. 500 to Rs. 600 annually.[12] This system of levying tax at Rs. 15 per one hundred logs was changed later on and the rate was increased to Rs. 4 and annas 4 per axe used for felling trees.[13] Thus, the awareness of the utility of timber and other produces of the forest as a source of earning revenue became more and more intense as the need for finance increased to the British Government. Indian teak, which turned out to be the most durable and most sought after for ship-building, was used extensively for the Royal Navy in the Anglo-French wars of the early nineteenth century, and by merchantships in the later period of maritime expansion. The teak forests of the Western Ghats were devastated, as much of Western Europe had been deforested by the sixteenth century. This led to the first instance of forestry in the form of reservation of teak forests in Malabar in 1806.

Introduction of Railways

It was a turning point in the history of Indian forestry when the railway network was introduced, in the last decades of the nineteenth century. This was in response to the needs of augmenting colonial trade after the so-called Sepoy mutiny and to enable the export and import of primary commodities and finished goods. Within the span of fifty years between 1860 and 1910 railway track increased from 1349 kms. to 51,658 kms.[14] The expansion of railway network in India was a costly proposition as wooden sleepers had to be imported from Norway. This threw open a vast market for British manufactures and it provided a surplus British capital in seeking outlets abroad. There was wanton destruction of forests, especially during the early years of railway expansion and this led to an unprecedented assault on the more accessible forests just to meet the demands of railway sleepers. No provision was exercised over the felling operations and great chunks of forests were uselessly felled whose logs could not be utilized. The worst hit areas were the sub-Himalayan forests of

Kamrup, Nowgong and Lakhimpur districts where even other-than-sal trees were not spared. The British Forest Policy was primarily formulated to earn as much revenue as possible in complete disregard to the destruction and denudation of the pristine forests.

It was in this situation, that the colonial authorities were finally disillusioned to the fact that India's forests were not inexhaustible. Forest administration, which had so far suffered a "melancholy failure", due to lack of proper care was now accorded a place of primary administrative importance. The Governor General, Lord Dalhousie, while commenting on the early attempts at forest conservation in 1862, observed, "the subject of forest conservancy is an important administrative question". (Jameson, Unpublished). The railways were built to facilitate both troop movement and trade. Finally, the need was felt to establish a separate department, which would ensure a sustained availability of timber to meet the enormous requirements of railway sleepers. For the new Forest Department to function effectively, as Gadgil and Guha pointed out, what was required was a legislation that curtailed the hitherto unrestricted access of rural communities to forest. Ten years after the British had first issued a memorandum which regulated the movement of forest dwellers within the forests of India, the Indian Forest Act of 1865 was introduced. The Act empowered the Government to appropriate to itself any land covered with trees, as "reserves" land on condition that the notification for government intention to reserve the land, could be acted upon only if the existing rights of the individuals and communities were not infringed upon. This was the first ever comprehensive piece of legislation that gave East India Company the right over the forests of India. The process of constituting reserved forests under the provision of this Act went on headlong in various districts of Assam. This large-scale reservation of forests by the Colonial government constituted a decisive turning point for the people of Assam politically, socially and ecologically. Politically, because the statutory claim laid by the government to the forests wealth of Assam represented an unjust appropriation of peoples possession and deprival of their legitimate rights; Socially, because the process caused a breach of traditional customs and usages of the Assamese people; and ecologically, because it amounted to human interference on the natural flora and fauna. At the initial stage the task of Imperial Forest management was entrusted to Mr. Gustav Mann, as Assistant Conservator of Forests, since Britain itself had no tradition of managing forests for timber production. Later on in 1874 when Assam was reconstituted into a Chief Commissioner's province Mr. Mann was promoted to the post of Deputy Conservator of Forests. It was a difficult task indeed, in those days, to ensure an effective enforcement of legislation that would seemingly run counter to the traditional rights of the villagers and tribal communities.[15] While, by and large, the British followed a *laissez-faire* policy that allowed the villagers to freely roam about in the forests and utilize its produce, there is also definite evidence from certain areas that "all land of every description was kept open even for absolute right to the community, subjects only to the yearly payment of rent fixed." (Superintendent Dehradun, to Commissioner, Meerut Division, dated:22.5.1897, No. 1997/iv a-244 of 1897) File No. 244 List No. 2 (UPRA).

Indian Forest Act of 1865, the first Forest Act of India, was replaced thirteen years later by another Indian Forest Act of 1878 which was more stringent and comprehensive. The provisions of the 1878 Act were to serve as a model not only for India but for other British colonies as well, but, while some officials within the colonial administration were sharply critical of the new legislation, calling it an Act going against the customary usage of forest by Indian people, their objections were swiftly overruled by the government.

Dietrich Brandis was appointed as the First Inspector General of Forests, who was credited to have laid the foundations of modern forestry in India; in fact, he was often paid the tribute as the "Father of Indian Forestry". Mr. Brandis was a botanist from Bonn University and Germany was considered as the leading European country in Forest Management of the time. One of the first tasks undertaken by the newly formed Forest Department was to survey and map out the forests of India.

According to the 1878 Forest Act, forests were categorised into three types—Reserved forest, Protected forest and Village Reserved forests. These three classes of forests were deemed to be the most commercially valuable and hence susceptible to sustained exploitation. Overall state control of reserved forests was sought, which involved either the relinquishment or infringement of people's claims and rights, although limited access was granted. Legally, provisions were open to public to contest the reservation of forests, though rural communities had little experience with legal procedures, and illiterate villagers were often unaware that a survey and demarcation was in process for reservation of forests. Protected forests were similarly state controlled, but some concessions were granted, conditional to the reservation of commercial tree species, when they became valuable. Protected forests could also be closed to fuelwood collection and grazing, whenever it was deemed necessary to do so. As demand for timber increased in the country and it was found that the state had limited capability to meet the requirement, the protected forests were upgraded to reserved forests. The Act also provided for constitution of third category of forests called the Village forests—though according to Gadgil and Guha (1992), this was not done by the colonial government over most part of India. The area of forest appropriated by the State in 1878 was estimated at 14,000 square miles, which had increased to 81,400 of Reserved forest and 3,300 square miles of Protected Forests by 1900[16]. The framework of the 1878 Act was designed basically to cater to the strategic imperial needs at that time—the supply of large scale timber for the railways. Some of the provisions of the Indian Forest Act 1878 ensured the following objectives:

1. The state could demarcate valuable tracts of forest needed especially for railways purposes.
2. Retain enough flexibility over the remaining extent of forest land to revise its policy from time to time.
3. Monopoly right was established by a legal sleight of hand, which sought to establish that the customary use of the forest by the villagers, based not on 'right' but on 'privilege' and that 'privilege' was exercised only at the mercy of the local rulers (the British were then the local rulers).
4. There were provisions for demarcation of 'Reserved' and 'Unreserved' forests with a list of reserved trees being drawn. Persons were to be notified to record their claims over land and forest produce in the proposed reserved and unreserved forests.

Consequences of the Indian Forest Act, 1878

The most immediate consequence of the Indian Forest Act of 1878 was visible in the discontented minds of the forest communities, who now totally lost control over their habitat. This evolved a sharp reaction from the forest communities who rose in popular revolts in an attempt to restore a 'golden past' where the tribal roamed freely in his forest habitat. What was even worse, was the sense of alienation that the forest dwellers were made to feel towards their own home, the forest to which they were attached. This feeling of alienation further started weakening the link between the people and the forest. Commenting on the attitude of the villagers of Jaunsar Bawar towards the forest settlement, the Superintendent of Dehradun said: "Not altogether without reason, the villagers believe that any self-denial or trouble they may exercise is preserving and improving their third class forests, will end in appropriation of the forests by the (forest) department as soon as they become commercially valuable".[17] The anthropologist Verrier Elwin too has talked about the melancholy effect forest renovation had on the tribals of Middle India, for whom nothing aroused more resentment against the government than the taking away of the forests they regarded as 'their own property'.[18]

It was under such conditions of discontentment and anguish of the people, that a series of untoward events, conflicts and struggles manifested centering around the question of forests. To cite an example, even the "timid and submissive" Garos, a matrilineal tribal community of the Garo Hills, resented the British over-lordship and joined their brethren in a movement for its dereservation. After the Government of Assam considered the question of forest reservation in Garo Hills in 1879, one Mr. Fisher was deputed with the rank of an Assistant Conservator of Forest, in 1881. His report based on an extensive tour of the Hills, formed the basis of forest conservancy. However, there were many cases filed by the Garos and one prominent Garo leader Sonaram Sangma was briefly imprisoned. Out of desperation, Sonaram Sangma and about one lakh Garos addressed a memorandum to Lord Minto, the Viceroy and Governor General of India, in February 9, 1906. They petitioned that their ancestors had enjoyed the privilege of living in the forests in the Garo Hills, made use of the forest products, sold them for their benefit besides cultivating and having rights of pasturage. With the passing of the Indian Forest Act VII of 1865 and 1878 and its subsequent enactments, they had been deprived of their age-old privilege and advantages without having been compensated in any way[19]. The social unrests manifested in different tribal areas thus evoked a sharp people's reaction to forest administration. This brought a disparity between the revenue and law and order administration on the one hand and the forest department on the other. There also grew a sharp criticism about the exclusion of agrarian population from the benefits of forest management.

The colonial approach to forestry was then reformed in 1894, on the advice of the German Agricultural Chemist Dr. J.A. Voelcker, who stressed the importance of good forest cover to avoid environmental degradation which, otherwise, might impact upon taxable agricultural output. The new legislation generated out of this advice came to be known as the 'Voelcker Resolution' according to which the forest administration was reviewed and followed. Dr. Voelcker in his report mainly emphasised on the improvement of agriculture and recommended that government should "direct the policy of the forest department so that it shall serve agricultural interest more directly than at present". Criticizing the objectives of the Forest Department, Dr. J.A. Voelcker, an Agricultural Chemist stated in his report *Improvement of Indian Agriculture*, 1893:

> "The forest department's objects were in no sense agricultural, and its success was gauged mainly by fiscal consideration; the department was to be revenue paying one. Indeed, we may go so far as to say that its interests were opposed to agriculture, and its intent was rather to exclude agriculture than to admit it to participate in its benefits."

The forest department was criticized for not serving the interests of the rural population in general and agrarian population in particular. Dr. Voelcker, while stating an alternative solution to this, advocated the creation of "Fuel and Fodder Reserves". He justified this policy on the grounds that in the long run any "possible diminution" of forest revenue may be attended by increased revenue to the state from cultivated land.

Accordingly, the Inspector General of Forests reviewed the principles of forest administration during 1892-93. The Review of Forest Administration of the Inspector General of Forests, 1892-93 states—

> "The sole object with which state forests are administered is the public benefit. In some cases the public to be benefited are the whole body of taxpayers; in others, the people of the tracts within which the forest is situated; but in almost all cases the constitution and preservation of a forest involve, in greater or less degree, the regulation of rights and the restriction of privileges of user in the forest area which may have previously been enjoyed by the inhabitants of its immediate neighbourhood".[20] Besides, the forest was broadly classified into the following groups:

(a) Forests the preservation of which is essential on climatic or physical grounds.
(b) Forests which afford a supply of valuable timbers for commercial purposes.
(c) Minor forests.
(d) Pasture lands.

The above grouping of forests indicates that Commercial production of timber was the main policy thrust, but some concessions to the ecological function of forest and pasture lands were also tacitly acknowledged. This revised principle consequently served as a model for forest policies in other colonies also.

The reorganization of a Forest Department as per opinion of Dr. Voelcker might have been desirable from a financial and agricultural points of view but it did promote a great amount of irritation in various parts of India. The Indian Forest Act, 1878 came to be identified as the general law relating to forest in British India, though it suffered from ambiguity in its provisions up to 1947, the administration of forest "estate" of British India was centred around imperial interests. During the period of railway expansion, India's forests proved to be important source of raw materials in the imperial scheme of things. The impact of the Second World War was more severely felt on the Indian forests. Timber and bamboo were supplied for construction of bridges, piers, buildings, huts and lines and ships.[21] India's forests were being requisitioned for imperial causes. Nevertheless, the Forest Department generated an adequate source of revenue to justify its existence and efforts were made to find markets for the rich and multiple species of India's tropical forest products. This was made possible by the requirements of urban centres for fuelwood, furniture, building materials, etc., while supply was facilitated by the improved communications, the railway network brought about ecological, economic and political impact on Assam. The British rulers were reluctant to limit the individual rights over forests and they sought to restrict only those rights, which were inconsistent with their material interests. The British Forest Policy was based on the assumption that the claims of forest preservation and commercial interest at the least deprivation of the forest-dwellers should be the sole objective.

The first completely published memorandum of the forests of Assam was included in the Resolution of the Government of Bengal on the 1869-70 report, dated 12th December 1870. However, the first mention made on the subject of conserving the forests was in the year 1850. In a report to the Commissioner, the Collector of Kamrup suggested that a tax should be levied on all timbers felled instead of allowing the timber contractors to fell indiscriminately where they pleased. Most of the wood carried from Bengal and had now made their appearance in Kamrup, in search of valuable species of trees such as sal timber, sal forests. As such, it was felt that a check should be established on the felling of young trees of valuable species in order to prevent waste and ensure the regeneration of the forests. The proposal was that the income derived from such taxes would reach a sum of Rs. 500 to Rs. 600 annually although the tax was a small one of Rs. 15 per 100 logs on the approval of the Commissioner and Deputy Governor of Bengal the new tax system was approved but it did not survive long. In the year 1852, the Board of Revenue abolished this system and a new policy system was introduced, which supported the cause of the farmers. This new policy was more common in other provinces of India where the farmers were left at liberty to weaken the forests they pleased provided they proved themselves to be the highest bidders for a period of five years.

The conservancy matters related to the new policy included certain orders that were the steps in the right direction, for example, in 1863, the Commissioner recommended that the fiscal officers should protect the forests from spoliations and prevent the felling of small trees of certain noted species. Another step taken was the preservation of Nambor Forest and the deputation of Forest Officers.

It was in the year 1868 that a new revenue system was introduced under which the Mouzadars (small tahsildars) were given the charge of forest and their protection. The appointment of an Assistant Conservator of Forests Mr. Gustav Mann who was specially deputed for preparing a general map of all the forests in the lower provinces of Bengal was another important step. This inspection commenced at the Sunkosh Rivers, the western boundary of the Province north of the Brahmaputra and was carried out during the years 1868-69 and 1869-70, the results being recorded in the Annual Forest Administration Reports of Bengal for these years.

In what was supposed to be an adequate protection to the forests or realizing the proper revenue from them, the 1868 Revenue System too proved a failure. The First Annual Progress Report of Assam, prepared by the Assistant Conservator, Mr. Gustav Mann in 1874-75 projected certain loopholes in the Revenue System. Most of the valuable sal forests were being felled, forests were devastated and it was the Mouzadars who were making a lucrative business out of it. Over and above this, two saw mills Deehing and Dibrugarh, were working in the forests and the Mouzadars who were actually supposed to be the guardians for the government's interest, were themselves supplying timber to the saw mills. The advent of the tea industry also proved to be a great cause of threat to the forests of Assam as large areas of natural forest lands were deforested for cultivation of tea. This also posed a real problem to the forest department as to which classes of forest land might be sold or leased out for tea industry.

Under this backdrop, the era of forest conservancy slowly dawned over Assam when government examined selection, classification of Assam forest. The Reports of the Assistant Conservator, Mr. Gustav Mann noted that the forest areas of Assam reached the 7800 square miles mark, including vast areas of *jhum* cultivation in tribal belts, such as Garo Hills and also excluded grassland areas with scattered trees over them.

Forest Operations in Assam After June 1873

In June 1873, Mann submitted to the Commissioner a memorandum of proposed forest operations in Assam. At the same time, Schlich, Conservator of Forests, Bengal and Assam was touring in Assam and the Commissioner asked the Conservator if he would give him the benefit of his advice on the memorandum. Schlich drew up a memorandum embodying his views regarding forest operations in Assam, dated 10th July, 1873. This memorandum is of high interest, since it displays the position from which the whole matter was regarded by the Commissioner and the Conservator.

The salient points of forestry proposals for Assam and comments forwarded by Schlich are shown in the following records:

(1) The total land under forest cover should be brought up to an area of 700 square miles, the rest of the forest areas being left entirely open, only sal, rubber and soom (*Machilus odd ratissima*) should be declared as reserved trees.

(2) He also laid stress on the policy for plantations and protecting of rubber or casutchouc.

(3) Schlich's records indicate that the first step towards forest conservancy in Assam started from the reservation of Nambor Forest in the Sibsagar District during the time when Colonel Jenkins was Commissioner of Assam.

(4) Experimental plantations were carried out on teak at several established stations. Experimental plantations had been established at a place adjacent to the Kulsi River (July 1872) in Khasi Hills, and at Makoom, on the Deehing River in Assam. However, the plantation at Makoom was almost a failure about which Schlich thought that the cold and dampness of Upper Assam was possibly the reason.

(5) Schlich was not very optimistic about the possibilities of Assam forests from the revenue point of view, although he felt that Assam was provided with much more timber and wood than was likely to be required for local use. This opinion made by him was primarily due to two major problems—firstly, there were no adequate transport and communication system in Assam, and secondly there was great problem of

scarcity of labour. The local Assamese people were not willing to work in the forest due to unhealthy climate and labour had to be hired from outside the province.

There were, however, good prospects for conserving and extending the pine forests of Upper Khasi Hills. Schlich was particularly interested in the rubber production, which was one of the most important and, at the same time, neglected subjects of the forests department of Assam. The high commercial value of this article had led to ruining the trees by over tapping and smuggling without proper supervision. Schlich was of the view that collection of rubber should be made free but revenue should be levied on rubber by imposing an export duty. Keeping in view of the high potential of rubber cultivation for revenue earning in Assam it was proposed to create a Government monopoly in management and production of rubber. This was also the opinion of the Commissioner of Assam.

On the subject of labour supply, Schlich's memorandum was in favour of paying wages at the current rate to every coolie (local labour) who came to work and giving them perfect liberty to leave the job when they liked, a policy which was adopted by Mr. Aylmer, the then forest officer in lower Assam.

(5) The other question, which Schlich considered, was in connection with the Soom (*Machilus odoratissuria*) forests and the silkworm industry. Schlich did not consider that the Revenue Department should interfere because the out-turn of silk product comes from the forest and therefore it should be credited as forest revenue. To this, the Commissioner took the strongest objection stating that as the Revenue Authorities had created the industry they should benefit by the results of their labours.

In consideration of the 1874-75-forest report, a few cases were settled with regard to the forests of Cachar, which was then transferred to Assam. Accordingly, the first Annual Administrative Report on forest of Assam was drawn up for the year 1874-75 and the Chief Commissioner sanctioned the following five forest divisions for the province—(1) Goalpara, (2) Guwahati, (3) Tezpur, (4) Golaghat, (5) Cachar.

(1) *Goalpara*—The Goalpara Division comprised of the Government open forest in the Eastern Division of the Goalpara district, covering an area of 422 squaremiles, out of which, about 80 squaremiles were sal forests.

(2) *Guwahati*—The Gauhati Divi Reserves in the Kamrup District and the western half of the Nowgong District all of which, were sal forests.

(3) *Tezpur*—The Tezpur Division comprised Forest Reserves in the Darrang District covering an area of 179.59 square miles, out of which, only one square mile was sal forest, all the rest being mixed lower hill and mixed plain forests. This area included the Nowduar Reserves and the Charduar rubber plantation.

(4) *Golaghat*—Golaghat comprised the Nambor Reserve of 389.25 square miles in the Sibsagar and Naga Hills District and the Mikir Hills Reserve of 65 square miles in the eastern half of the Nowgong District.

(5) *Cachar*—The Cachar Division comprised an area of 825 square miles in the Cachar District and 273 square miles in the Sylhet District which it had been proposed to declare reserves under Act VII of 1865 to be managed by the Divisional Forest Officer.

A great many forests were constituted as Reserved Forests under section 2 of Act VII of 1865 until 1870. After the passing of the Indian Forest Act VII of 1878 all the existing Reserved Forests constituted under Act 1865 were regularised by re-notifying under Section 34. In 1891 the Assam Forest Regulation VII was promulgated and since that time new Reserved Forests were notified under Section 2 of that Regulation. According to this Regulation the local government might constitute any land at the disposal of the government as Reserved Forest through publication of a notification in the Official Gazette. Any complaint against the notification was to be settled by the Forest Settlement Officer to be appointed for that purpose. After the disposal of the complaint by the Forest Settlement Officer the Deputy Commissioner of the district concerned might issue notification in vernacular declaring the constitution of the Reserved Forest.

The Government of India came up with another forest Act in 1927 by the nomenclature, Act XVI Act of 1927 with a view to remove some ambiguities that were found in Act 1878 in the process of working in the provinces outside Assam. Thus, it was replaced by the enactment of the Indian Forest Act 1927, which incorporated the provisions of other existing Acts and made the Forest Act more clear and comprehensive. This Act repealed the Indian Forest Act VII, 1878, the Indian Forest Act V, 1901, the Indian Forest (Amendment) Act XV, the Indian Forest Amendment Act, 1918, and the Devolution Act XXXVIII, 1920, and it remained as the only workable forest Act of the British until Independent India came up with her new forest policy in 1952. However, in respect of Assam the Assam Forest Regulation of 1891 was found to be suitable and hence it continued to be the major forest Act.

The Indian Forest Act, 1927, was indeed, a very comprehensive Act including all earlier amendments and major provisions of the Acts enacted before 1927. Among the major features of the Act, the most important provisions that affected the public relations were as follows:

(a) The Forest Act, 1927, omitted wrongful arrests as provided in the previous Acts of 1865 and 1878.
(b) The provisions relating to community rights over forest were abrogated by the 1927 Act.

In the Act of 1927, important terms about forest are defined as follows:

Forest-produce means—

(a) Any forest produce, whether found in or brought from a forest or not, that is to say: timber, charcoal, cautchouc, catechu, wood-oil, resin, natural varnish, lac, mahua-flowers, mahua-seeds, kuthand myrabolams, and
(b) When found in or brought from a forest:
    (1) Trees and leaves, flowers and fruits, and all other parts or produce not hereinbefore mentioned of trees;
    (2) Plants not being trees (including grasses, creepers, reeds and moss), and all parts or produce of such plants;

(3) Wild animals and skins, tusks, horns, bones, silk, cocoons, honey and wax and all other parts or produce of animals;
(4) Peat, surface soil, rock and minerals (including limestone, laterite, mineral oils and all products of mines or quarries);
(5) "River" includes any stream, canal, creek or other channels, natural or artificial;
(6) "Timber" includes trees when they have fallen or have been felled, and all wood whether cut up or fashioned or hollowed out for any purpose or not; and
(7) "Tree" includes palms, bamboos, stumps, brushwood and canes.

The Act also provided that the State Government might constitute any forest-land or waste-land which is the property of the Government or over which the government has proprietary rights, or to the whole or any part of the forest-produce to which the Government is entitled.

Forest Village

The Forest Department of Assam established a number of Forest Villages in the peripheries of Reserved Forests for the purpose of proper maintenance of the forests. The origin of Forèst Village begins from the days of British. The Indian Forest Act, 1878 provided for the Constitution of forest village for within the forest itself the purpose of obtaining daily labourers required to work in the forest. Later on the Assam Forest Regulation, 1891 further regularized the system of management of forest villages which gave the local government the power to make rules for regulating the nature and extent of forest village, the rights and responsibilities of Labourers living in the forests. The necessity of Constitution of forest village was prompted by the acute problem of obtaining labourers in Assam. It was often commented that "the Assamese were unwilling to do any work if they could avoid it".[22] Moreover, during the seasons of planting and harvesting of paddy it was very difficult to obtain labour for hire. After Independence forest villages have begun springing up rapidly as the area and number of Reserved forests increased and work of afforestation and protection of new forest areas also increased. As per the provisions of the Act, a limited number of forest villages were allowed to be located inside the reserved forests to house the labourers needed for family was entitled to 8 hectares of land to clear[23] and cultivate and also to keep 5 heads of cattle, while each adult forest villager was required to render twenty days labour per annum at the rate of wages prevailing in that locality. Every family was entitled to building materials to erect and maintain their house free of royalty and ten cart loads of fuel annually if they elected to render ten days labour equal to royalty.

One problem that arose out of this provision of the Indian Forest Act had been the unprecedented growth of forest villages in and around the reserved forests. Most of them living within the forest village worked outside the forest but utilized the benefits of tax exemption to their advantage. There was only two ways to solve this problem and these were—either to enhance the rate of wages at par with that prevailed in the locality or to maintain strict vigilance to make sure that the labourers render work up to the stipulated number of days.

Colonial Forestry in the Khasi Hills

British rule marks an important watershed in the hitherto secluded natural ecology of the Khasi and Jaintia Hills. A new phase of human management of forests in the Khasi Hills began immediately following the visit of Lord Northbrook, the Viceroy of India, to the Khasi Hills in 1874. The British Government took up steps to reserve a number of forest tracts for the purpose of regeneration and preservation of timber trees. Within a short period of time as many as thirty-seven 'Reserved' and 'Protected' forests, varying in sizes from 0.65 to 18 sq. kms. were constituted in several of the then Khasi states.[24]

In addition, a number of 'Green Blocks' for protecting the water supply of Shillong and providing firewood were also set up in the neighbourhood of the town including:

1. The Laitumkhrah-Laitkor Block (I) and Block (II).
2. Riat Laban and Kenches' Trace.

3. Barapani Forest.
4. Upper Shillong A Tree Nursery Reserve.

Much of the areas lying within Block (I) and (II) was, however, dereserved in the early 1950's by the then Government of Assam for residential purposes.

The use of political supremacy by the colonial rulers as a source of power also paved the way for an absolute control over the natural resources in the country as a whole. However, the colonial policies concerning natural resources, varied in nature and extent across the length and breadth of India. It may be said with a sense of relief that the North Eastern region in general and the Khasi Hills in particular were excluded from full scale application of colonial land use policy. The hill areas of the North-East region being Excluded and Partially Excluded areas had a different story to tell in terms of degree of Imperial control.[25] Inaccessibility to the hills due to difficult terrain was a serious constraint which tended to restrict timber exploitation to areas on the route of navigable rivers. Originally, the timber was cut near the river sides so that they could be floated manually or dragged to the bank with the help of elephants and buffaloes.[26]

The forests in the hilly regions of the Khasi and Jaintia Hills were replete with *Pinus kesiya* (Khasi pine), which for centuries served the needs of local demands in timber and firewood. The *Asiatic Journal* Vol. XXI, September-December 1836, London reports that in Cherrapunji, the cost of firewood for burning lime was priced at four rupees eight *annas* only as compared to the areas which were furnished with tracts for its conveyance, where beams of twenty feet long and nine inches square cost six rupees each. With the price increasing to six rupees each, depending upon the difficulty of conveyance. Thus, if the Kasyas were provided with hill- tracks for its conveyance, large timber might be carried into use for cutting planks; a saw mill might take advantage from part of such a concern and should recommend to be established at Cherra. Despite Colonial efforts to export such timber to the plains there was very little prospect for utilizing the surplus stock of timber and carry out export trade because the expenditure in removing timber from these hills was too high in proportion to its value.

In yet another series, the Asiatic Journal Vol. XXI, September-December, 1836, London, informs of Cherrapunji's natural endowments: "The discovery of apparently inexhaustible mines of coal in almost immediate vicinity of navigable rivers must be considered as one of the most fortunate circumstances that could have occurred. A range of hills extending about three miles to the north and south, across the land between Cherra and Nongkhlaw, covers from summit to the base with fine timber and luxuriant vegetation, forms grand emporium of treasures."

Early efforts towards forest conservancy were not an easy task. As the Chief Commissioner, Colonel Keatinge said, "it is a very difficult thing to change the habits of a population, or to induce them to incur even a very small temporary inconvenience for a future benefit." The realization of the true objects of forest conservancy could only come slowly through the education of the people. This has been true in the case of the Khasis. As early as 1874-75, measures had been taken to put a stop to the indiscriminate burning of the forests in the Khasi and Jaintia Hills through extensive *jhuming*. These measures met with some success but the interference of village offers asked the Khasi "*siems*" over the conservancy of sacred groves came in their way. Other factors which had some influence in destroying the accessible forests in the Khasi and Jaintia Hills were the working of lime and also coal for local consumption in the stations of Shillong (elevation 4951 feet) and Cherrapunji. Iron smelting was also being carried on in the western portion of the Khasi Hills, and the denudation of the forests on these hills was to some extent attributable to the extensive manufacture of charcoal used for this industry, a result which had occurred in other parts of India.

According to the Assam District Gazetteers, 1915, the district forest administration was reorganized in 1907 with a separate office under the Deputy Commissioner. The staff consisted of one ranger, one forester, and one headguard and 14 permanent guards. The following Table 3.1 presents the revised list of protected forest in the Khasi Hills.

The Jirang forest has not been included in the list of protected forests as it was leased to the government in perpetuity by the Agreement of 1859. The Assam District Gazetteer, 1914, also stated some important informations regarding the land area, forest and

Table 3.1: Revised List of Protected Forests in the Khasi Hills

Sl. No.	State in which Situated	Name of Forest	Approx. Area in Sq.m.
1.	Cherra	Mawphan Siem	1¾
2.	-do-	Thynriewsiar	¼
3.	-do-	Ka Lyngkper	¼
4.	Khyrim	Lum Masur	½
5.	Nongsohphoh	Kulailyngsngun	6¼
6.	Maharam	Lawblei	½
7.	-do-	Sakuang	1½
8.	-do-	Nongkdait or Ryngbneng	8½
9.	-do-	Rangmaw	1
10.	Mariaw	Ka Miangsain near Nongkasen	¾
11.	-do-	Langkrai	½
12.	-do-	Tersung	1
13.	Mawiang	Mar Shillong	1½
14.	-do-	Lawsain	1¼
15.	Mawsynram	Mawsynram	1½
16.	Mylliem	Mawreng	3¼
17.	-do-	Mawpat	1
18.	-do-	Umtru	2¼
19.	-do-	Umtan	1½
20.	Nongkhlaw	Tersung	1
21.	-do-	Law Synïong near Mawnaipunji	1½
22.	-do-	Mairang Forest	¼
23.	-do-	Mairang Forest	¼
24.	Nongspung	Nongspung	¾
25.	-do-	Lyngkhoi Forest	¼
26.	Nongstoin	Nongstoin Forest	4½
27.	Rambrai	Mawdoh Forest	7
28.	Mawphlang	Umkawang	¼
29.	Mawphlang & Nonglwai	Khlaw Ryngisohlong	1
30.	Nonglwai	Khlaw Mawkaleng	½
31.	Sohïong	Law Sohïong	¼
32.	-do-	Law Nongkseh	2¾
33.	Laitlyngkot	Laitlyngkot (Mun)	2¼
34.	Laitkroh	Laitkroh	¾
35.	Mawsmai	Kyrnah Ka Dier	¼
36.	Nonglang	Nongkynah	¾

Source: Assam District Gazetteers, 1915.

agriculture and administration in the hills, particularly in the newly constituted Municipality—Shillong.

The Shillong Municipality and Reserved Forests

Shillong, the summer hill station of Assam in the Khasi Hills was constituted as a station under Act V (B.C.) of 1876 in 1878 and afterwards converted into a Municipality under Act III of 1884 in November 1910. Its affairs are managed by a committee of 15 members presided over by the Deputy Commissioner. The principal sources of revenue are a tax on houses at 7½ per cent of the annual rental, water and latrine rates and a grant from government.

The total area of the town including the cantonment was about 8 square miles and it is served by about 20 miles of metalled and nearly 8 miles of unmetalled roads. An excellent supply of drinking water was obtained from springs rising in the Shillong range and was distributed in pipes all over the town.

In the neighbourhood of Shillong, three other forest areas were connected into a game preserve in 1906—(1) Laitkor, (2) Wahrisa, (3) Riat Laban.

The following forests were then brought under a regular working plan with effect from 1909-1910.

Name of Forest	*Acres*
Riat Khwan	967
Short Round	262
Laitkor	725
Upper Shillong	1,286
Riat Laban	430
Total	3.670

The cantonment forests comprising an area of 137 acres were also placed under a rough working plan system. In addition to this, the Kenche's Trace, the Laitumkhrah and Block II forests have been placed under the Shillong Municipality for the extension of the station.

During the colonial rule the region around Shillong was described as "undulating grassy country covered with scattered trees and occasional clips of wood and the whole scenery was park-like"[27] On the eastern side of the hills, there were "crowds of market people laden with dried fish, baskets full of birds, cherries, cinnamon, bark, iron, pine flakes, firewood and potato." It is also reported that extensive forests of the *Pinus longifolia* (*Pinus khasya*) are to be found adjacent to Shillong, but the Lieutenant Governor regrets to learn of their indifferent treatment by those who own them. The government was unable to interfere in the management of these private forests but the Commissioner's attention for his remarks regarding the condition of the forest would be called for. The suggestion was that the vast tracts of pine forests should be extended since the trees suffered from jungle fires. About seven square miles of land round Shillong belonged to the government and contained some quality pine forests on it. Efforts were made to preserve those lands which were covered with *Pinus khasya* and also other lands covered with evergreen and exotic broad-leaved trees. A considerable number of seedlings of oaks, chestnut, walnut and several species of *Eucalyptus, Casuarina*, various European pines, W. Himalayan conifers were also raised and planted in and around Shillong. All these plantation works progressed favourably and a few exotic species like *Juglans regia, Eucalyptus rostrata* and *Piris maritama* showed good results and some of these plantations can still be seen today in some of the suburbs of Shillong city.

Notes

1. Arnold David and Guha.
2. Choube, S.K., *Hill Politics in Northeast India*, 1973, pp. 23-24.
3. Stern, Klaus and *et al.*, *Genetics of Forest Ecosystem*, pp. 210ff.
4. Brandis, D., Suggestion Regarding the Forest Administration in Assam, p. 3.
5. Baruah, S.L., *A Comprehensive History of Assam*, p. 241.
6. Gadgil, M. and Guha, *The Fissured Land: An Ecological History of India*, p. 119.
7. Ribbentrop, B., *Forest in British India*, p. 52.
8. Gadgil, M. and Guha, R. *The Fissured Land: An Ecological History of India*, p. 78.
9. *Assam Gazette*, 16 September, 1876, Part II of Forest Rules.
10. Ribbentrop, B., *Forestry in India*, p. 60.
11. Stebbing, 1923-26.
12. Mann Gustv, Progress Report of Forest Administration in the Province of Assam, 1874-75, p. 1.
13. Barpujari, H.K., *Assam in the Days of the Company*, 1826-1858, p. 234.
14. Report of Government of India, 1964.
15. Guha and Gadgil, 1988.
16. Stebbing, 1892.

17. Sinha, A.C., 1988, p. 40.
18. Voelcker, 1897, p. 14.
19. Sinha, A.C., 1993, p. 115.
20. Circular No. 22-Forest, Dated 19th October, 1894.
21. Sinha, A.C., 1994, p. 59.
    Individuals were expected to file their claims on forest land and forest produce before the Forest Settlement Officer (FSO), who was to enquire into these claims. Rights in respect of which no claims were preferred were to be extinguished unless the individual claiming them satisfied the Forest Settlement Officer.
22. Coventry, E.M., Working Plan for the Reserved Forests of Nawgong Division, Eastern Bengal and Assam, 1909, p. 11.
23. Sinha, A.C., 1993, p. 59.
24. Allen, B.C., *Gazetteer of Khasi and Jaintia Hills*, Shillong, 1890, pp. 82-84
25. Singh. Daman, *The Last Frontier. People and Forest in Mizoram*, 1996, p. 38.
26. Sinha, A.C., *op. cit.* 1993, p. 62.
27. *Ibid.*, 1993.

4

Post Colonial History of Forestry in Khasi and Jaintia Hills

After India's Independence in 1947, the Khasi and Jaintia Hills district continued to remain as such within the State of Assam until 1970, when a new state was carved out on 2nd April, 1970 by the name Meghalaya and it was declared a full-fledged state of Indian Union on January, 21, 1972. The State of Meghalaya was constituted comprising two erstwhile districts of Assam, viz Khasi and Jaintia Hills district and Garo Hills district. A look into the post colonial forestry in Khasi and Jaintia Hills therefore covers two phases, out of which, the first phase includes forestry in Assam as a district and thereafter, till date, as part of Meghalaya State.

With the attainment of Independence, India came out with a Centrally Planned model of economic development which influenced the course of history of the forestry in India. The post colonial period was characterised by introduction of Five Year Plans that set out priority areas in each sector. Thrust areas in agriculture and animal husbandry were often found to reflect the dominant theme of planning in India. Five Year Plans to be implemented after Independence were mainly focused towards development of agriculture for making India self-sufficient in food production while the Second and Third Five Year Plans reflected a drive towards small and heavy industrialization.

Considerable administrative and legislative changes were brought in through intense drive for industrialisation under Nehru's vision of modernization. Such fundamental changes greatly impacted upon the forest resources of India. There were many factors that contributed to the acceleration of forest loss and deforestation. The changes in land tenure systems through enactment of Zamindari Abolition Acts and Government acquisition of land through Land Ceiling Act prompted the Zamindars and landlords to large-scale felling of trees on their lands for fear of nationalization. With the acceleration of economic development in the country the demand for timber required for construction and industrial uses increased which led to commercial exploitation of forests. Between the 1950's and 1970's millions of hectares of land were leased out to industries at heavily subsidized rates and were able to continue with unsustainable silvicultural practices subject to generous contributions to the politicians offers, who would then influence the Forest Department to turn a blind-eye[1].

There was a sharp increase in the production of industrial goods made out of wood leading to the rapid growth of forest based industries. The paper industry, for example, recorded an increase from 98,800 tonnes in 1948 to over one million tonnes in 1978.[2] Large scale forest lands were used for development of communication network reaching out to the far-flung rural areas and all-weather roads and major highways were built at the cost of forest lands. Thousands of hectares of lands covered with forests submerged under water in the name of giant dams and reservoirs for hydro-power projects and irrigation canals. Such a dynamic progress of economic development throughout the country leading to rapid decline in the forest cover heralded a new approach towards conservation of forest through large-scale plantations of quick growing, high yielding tree species, that would boost up rejuvenation of the dwindling ecology This could be clearly visible in the 1961 massive programme, which represented a significant departure from earlier forest management practices.

With the rapid exploitation of the forest resources there was the growing awareness that the dwindling natural forests have to be supplemented with biomass specially produced for industrial consumption. The thrust of the Second and Third Plans, therefore, were laid on the plantation of trees of fast growing species, such as eucalyptus and other indigenous varieties which could mature within a short period of time. New slogans like '*Van Mahotsava*' was coined for creating people's awareness about forest value and Tree plantation ceremonies were observed. Thus, by1980 over 2.2 million hectares of plantations had been grown.[3]

National Forest Policy of 1952

The policy instruments are the means by which the activities of government agencies and other institutions are directed towards the achievement of certain desired objectives. While framing such policies the concerned state departments are invariably consulted and their comments are incorporated before the desired objectives are finalised. The National Forest Policy, 1952 recognised forest under four categories, viz, (1) Protected Forests, (2) National Forest, (3) Village Forest and the (4) Private Forest. This was a revision of the National Forest Ploicy, 1865 adopted by the British Government and, therefore, it continued to consider forest as a source of revenue although economic development was given the top priority. The policy envisaged maximum utilisation of the existing natural resources of the country for the purpose of all round development and upliftment of society from illiteracy, poverty, hunger and disease. These objectives were sought to be achieved by harnessing all the resources of the country such as, the land, water, forest, bio-diversity, and mineral resources. The following extract from the National Forest Policy, 1952 will substantiate this assumption.

> "Village communities in the neighbourhood of forest will naturally make greater use of its products for the satisfaction of their domestic and agricultural needs. Such use, however, should in no event be permitted at the cost of national interest. The accident of a village being situated close to a forest does not prejudice the right of the country as a whole to receive the benefits of a national asset" — "Restrictions should be imposed in the interests not only of the existing generation but also of posterity."[4]

The framers of the National Forest Policy derived guidance from the following directive principles laid down at the Sixth Conference of FAO held in 1951.

It says :-

(a) Each country should determine and set aside areas to be dedicated to Forest whether at present forested or not.
(b) Each country should apply the best practicable techniques in seeking to derive the maximum benefits available from the protective, productive and accessory values of its forests.
(c) Adequate knowledge of all aspects of forest resources and forest and forest management including consumption and utilisation of forest produce indispensable.
(d) Public consciousness of forest values should be developed by all means.

The post colonial period saw the continued control over management of forests and utilization of resources by the administrators, which was nothing but a true imprint of its colonial past. The policy of 'Forest for Revenue' adopted by the colonial rulers was replaced by 'Forest for Development' and both of them contributed towards exploitation of forest resources at the cost of valuable ecological balance.

In March 1950, the Government of India set-up a Planning Commission to prepare a plan for the most effective and sustainable utilization of the country's resources. The Planning Commission has since been functioning as the kingpin of national development.

The various Five-Year Plans have, in consonance with the National Policy, laid emphasis on accelerating development of forest and creating fresh avenues for its expansion. The works carried out under various plans are:

The First Five Year Plan (1951-56) was launched at a time when the two world wars had drawn upon heavily on the forest resources. Major river valley projects industrial development defence and other projects vital for the development of the country also relied heavily upon forests and forest areas. Thus, the first plan encompassed all these aspects while taking into account the further development of forests and forestry. Under this plan, emphasis was laid upon the following points:

1. Ensuring that the production of both fuelwood and fodder is maintained to meet the growing needs of the people.

2. Attaining a maximum sustained yield of timber for railways, defence, industries and the common man.
3. Rehabilitation of forests, which had been over exploited in the two world wars.
4. To raise plantation for industries.

During the period of Second Plan (1956-61), emphasis was laid on the survey, demarcation and rehabilitation of forest degraded areas and development of the degraded forests. Priorities were also given to prevention of soil erosion, forest plantation and increase of timber yield for railways, defence and industries.

During the Third and the Fourth Plan period, special attention was paid on increasing production of timbers through plantation of fast growing species particularly for the pulp and paper industries. The Third Plan also saw the introduction of the Indian Forest Service in 1966 with a view to providing better and effective technical supervision in forest conservation and development activities all over India. An important event that took place during the Fourth Plan was to appoint the National Commission on Agriculture in 1970, which presented its report in 1976. The Commission recommended launching of massive social forestry programme in order to meet the growing requirement of timber, fodder and fuelwood to the community. Social forestry schemes were, thus, extended all over India through foreign aids like the World Bank, Swedish International Development Authority, the U.S. Agency for international development, etc.

During the Fifth Five Year Plan period the Government of India took a significant step by inclusion of Social Forestry programmes in the "20-Point Programme for Economic Development". Forest was also included in the concurrent list with a view to giving special attention under the supervision of the Central Government. Till date forest like agriculture was a subject of State Government. In the hill areas, like Khasi and Jaintia Hills, Naga Hills, Mizo Hills and North Cachar Hills of the North East, Autonomous District Councils were set-up under Sixth Schedule of the Constitution in 1952 and the task of control and management of forests was entrusted on them for the benefit of the tribal people. In the following paragraphs we shall briefly deal with the Constitution and functions of the Autonomous District Council in Khasi and Jaintia Hills district.

District Council and Forest Administration

After India's Independence, there was a rising demand among the hill tribes of Assam for protecting tribalism and a 'quest for identity' and, therefore, it became inevitable to grant them some kind of autonomy in their internal administration.[5] With a view to satisfying the aspirations of the tribal organisations in protecting and developing their tribal culture and identity the Constituent, Assembly of India made provisions for local self-government through Autonomous District Councils in each hill district under the Sixth Schedule of the Constitution. Accordingly, in 1952 the Khasi and Jaintia Hills Autonomous District Council was constituted with elected and nominated members as per Paragraph 2 of the Sixth Schedule. Under the provisions of the Sixth Schedule the District Councils were conferred with the power to legislate and execute on the following subjects :[6]

(a) The allotment, occupation or use, or the setting apart of land, other than that of the state's reserved forests, for the purpose of agriculture, grazing or other purposes in the interest of the inhabitants of any village, subject to the Assam Government's power to acquire land for public purposes.
(b) The management of any forest not being a reserve forest.
(c) The use of any canal or water course for the purpose of agriculture.
(d) The regulation of practice of Jhum or other forms of shifting cultivation.
(e) The establishment of village or town committee or council and their powers.
(f) Any other matter relating to village or town administration including village or town police and public health and sanitation.
(g) The appointment or succession of chiefs or headmen.
(h) The inheritance of property. marriage and divorce.
(i) Social customs.

As per power invested by Paragraph 5 of the Sixth Schedule, the Khasi and Jaintia Hills District Council took over the management and control of all the forests within the district. The term mentioned as 'Reserved Forest' in Paragraph 3(a) of the Sixth Schedule means that any area which is a reserved forest under the Assam Forest Regulation,1891 or under any other law for the time being in force, in the area in question. Thus, the reserved forests already in existence were kept out of the jurisdiction of the District Councils and were left under the control of the state Forest Department of the Government of Assam. Consequently, the forests of Khasi and Jaintia Hills came under dual control of the District Council and the state Forest Department of Assam. The existing reserved forests, National Parks and other Government owned forests were left under the control of the State Forest Department while the rest of the forest areas were brought under the Autonomous District Councils. The bifurcation of forests on this principle resulted in disproportionate and lopsided burden of works between the two authorities. The State Forest Department with a team of well qualified and trained technical establishment had to deal with a small area of reserved forest measuring 1127.23 sq. km, while the Autonomous District Councils, with comparatively a handful of untrained manpower had to shoulder the burden of a large forest area consisting of 6250.68 sq. km. The Autonomous District Councils cannot afford to maintain adequate staff due to financial constraints. On principle, there was an understanding between the two agencies that they would work in close co-ordination and that the State Forest Department would extend necessary technical assistance to the District Councils as and when required. But, in practice this did not happen, instead, there prevailed a sense of misunderstanding and lack of co-ordination between them leading to mismanagement and large scale destruction of forests. This happened particularly in respect of Autonomous District Councils. As regards the reserved forests the total area under it remained stagnant because of absence of government land in Khasi and Jaintia Hills, while the District Councils were unable to constitute reserved forest due to non-existence of legal provision. Therefore, the two agencies had the following categories of forests under each:

Under State Forest Department

1. Reserved Forests.

2. National Parks.
3. Any other government forest.

Under Autonomous District Councils

1. Protected Forests.
2. Unclassed State Forests.
3. Village Forests.
4. Private Forests.

It will be pertinent, at this point, to know the forest areas of different classifications held by the three Autonomous District Councils of Meghalaya as well as by the State Forest Department. Table 4.1 gives us the details of the Meghalaya forest areas separately under State Forest Department and Autonomous District Councils, district-wise and category-wise.[7]

Table 4.1: Forest areas directly under the control of the State Forests, Department of Meghalaya

(a) Reserved Forests	712.15 sq.kms.
(b) Protected Forests	12.39 sq.kms.
(c) National Parks	399.482 sq.kms.
(d) Proposed Nonumiang & Gittingri Reserved Forests	2.71 sq.kms.
(e) Areas under Parks & Gardens	0.50 sq.kms.
Total – A	**1127.232 sq.km.**
(f) Forest areas in the campus of the North-Eastern Hill University	3 sq.kms. (approx.)
(g) Forest areas under Defence	4 sq.kms. (approx.)
Total – B	**7 sq.kms. (approx.)**

Classification of Forest Lands in Meghalaya

In Meghalaya, forest may be classified in a number of ways such as by composition, legal status, ownership, exploitation and functions (Sinha, 1993). However, as far as uses of the word forest is concerned, in Meghalaya it is found to be interpreted in the following three ways:

"Reserved Forest", "Protected Forest" and "Unclassed Forest".

Table 4.2: Forest areas under the control of the Autonomous District Councils

A. Jaintia Hills Autonomous District Council	
(a) Unclassed State Forests	1000 sq.kms. (approx.)
(b) Protected Forests	34.22 sq.kms. (approx.)
(c) Village Reserved Forests	3.49 sq.kms.
(d) Private/Community Forests	Extent of the area not known at present since survey records are not available
Total – C	**1037.71 sq.kms. (approx.)**
C. Khasi Hills Autonomous District Council	
(a) Unclassed State Forests	Nil
(b) Protected Forests	Nil
(c) Village Reserved Forests (d) Private/Community Forests	Extent of private forest areas under Mylliem Syiemship is estimated at 161.17 sq.kms. Extent of area under other Syiemship are not known at present since areas are not surveyed
Total – E	**161.17 sq.kms.**
B. Garo Hills Autonomous District Council	
(a) Unclassed State Forests	Nil
(b) Protected Forests	Nil
(c) Village Reserved Forests	208.50 sq.kms.
(d) Private/Community Forests	4843.30 sq.kms.
Total – D	**5051.80 sq.kms.**

Source: Development of Forest and Environment, Government of Meghalaya.

Reserved Forest (RF)

These forests are managed and directly controlled by the State Government. These areas are notified under the provisions of Indian Forest Act or the State Forest Acts having full degree of protection. In Reserved Forests all activities are prohibited unless permitted.

Protected Forest (PF)

These forests are notified under the provisions of Indian Forest Act or the State Forest Acts having limited degree of protection. In protected forest all activities are permitted unless prohibited.

Unclassed Forest (UF) or District Council Reserve Forest

These forests are not included in reserved or protected forests category and ownership status of such forests varies from state to state. In Meghalaya they are directly controlled and managed by the District Councils under the Sixth Schedule of the Indian Constitution. All private forests or village forests are included in the unclassed forest.

Table 4.3: Forest cover in Meghalaya at a glance

District-wise Forest cover (Meghalaya) (Area in Km^2), 2001

District	*Geographical area*	*Forest Cover*				*Scrub*
		Dense forest	Open forest	Total	Per cent	
East Garo HillsTH	2,603	1,038	2,737	3,775	84.79	8
South Garo HillsTH	1,849					
East Khasi HillsTH	2,820	997	1,553	2,550	90.43	29
Jaintia HillsTH	3,819	890	1,047	1,937	50.72	117
Ri BhoiTH	2,376	656	1,107	1,763	74.20	68
West Garo HillsTH	3,715	1,002	1,590	2,592	69.77	3
West Khasi HillsTH	5,247	1,098	1,869	2,967	56.55	34
Total	**22,429**	**5,681**	**9,903**	**15,584**	**69.48**	**259**

Source: State of Forest Report 2001.

Khasi Hills Autonomous District (Management and Control of Forests) Act, 1958

According to the above Act the Autonomous District Council has classified the land as follows:

Private Forests

These forests are owned and managed by an individual or clan or a joint clan. They are either grown or inherited in recognised private lands (*Ri Kynti*).

Green Block

These are forests belonging to an individual family or clan or joint clan and Raid lands already declared as Green Block by the

Government for aesthetic beauty and water supply of the town of Shillong and its suburbs.

Raid Forests

These are forests looked after by the heads of the Raid under the management of the local administrative heads.

District Council Reserved Forests

These are forests that may be so declared by the Executive Committee and shall be owned, managed, controlled by the Executive Committee.

Unclassed Forests

These are forests hitherto known as Unclassed State Forests before the commencement of the Constitution of India directly managed and controlled by the Government including any other forest(s) not falling within any of the above classification (KHADC, 1995).

The classification of forest lands by the Land Reforms Commission Report and the Khasi Hills Autonomous District Council (KHADC), showed that ownership, control and management is the community, clan or private. The exact size of such of these classified forest lands is not known.

The District Councils besides controlling and managing some forest lands are also given constitutional power to make laws over the tribal areas. The Act of 1980 passed by the District Council states that the Community, clan and private forests must be registered with details of ownership and boundaries; the trees and any forest products from these forests cannot be disposed of by way of sale, mortgage, base, gift or otherwise without the approval of the competent authority of the District Council. The application of disposal of trees or any produce must be routed through the traditional heads who shall forward to the Chief Forest Officer (CFO) of the District Council. The Act does not in any manner deal with the internal mechanism of rights of use of the common property. It is left to the traditional institutions.

Promulgation of Forest Acts and Rules

Ever since the British handed over the power and left India, the Government of Assam was merely following the forest laws introduced by the colonial rulers. The major British laws, applicable in those days, were the Indian Forest Act, 1927 and the Assam Forest Regulation VII of 1891. After the State of Meghalaya came into being in 1972 the Government of Meghalaya adopted the Assam Forest Regulation, 1891, with some modification for its application in the state under the title—Meghalaya Forest Regulation (Application and Amendment) Act, 1973". This Act empowers the government to constitute a Reserved Forest at any land under the disposal of the government in a manner provided therein; to hear and dispose of cases arising out of claims for jhum cultivation ; claim for right of way, right of water-course, right of pasture etc. It also deals with constitution of Forest Village and its regulations.

The Government of Meghalaya also felt the necessity for a legislation for the purpose of protection of natural environment and forest around the hills and valleys as there was large scale destruction of forest in the state. With this objective in view the government promulgated Meghalaya Tree Protection Act, 1976 which prohibits felling of without prior permission of the Forest Department. The Section 3 of this Act runs as follows:

"No person shall fell any tree or cause to be felled any tree in any land whether of his ownership or otherwise, except with the prior permission of the Divisional Forest Officer who may grant such permission subject to condition not inconsistent with the provision of this Act." The contravention of the Section 3 of theis Act shall entail a punishment with fine of rupees one thousand. Closely allied to this Act is the Meghalaya Protection of Catchment Areas Act, 1988 which prohibits felling of trees around the catchment areas of Shillong city. This Act is very important insofar as these chatchment areas around Shillong help conservation of rain water as the primary sources of drinking water for the city.

The Government of India introduced Wildlife (Protection) Act,1972 which was a step towards the strengthening of conservation of the flora and fauna of the country. Many years back during British time one such legislation existed by the name "Wild Birds and Animals Protection Act, 1912" which sought to provide protection to certain specified wild birds and animals in order to save them from extinction. The new Act passed by the Government of India provided much needed security to the lives of many varieties of birds and animals which were in the verge of extinction. The Wildlife Protection Act, 1972 was further amended in 1991 which broadened the scope of the law to include plants the Secton 17 of this amended Act prohibits "collection, cultivation, trading and dealing" with certain specified plants without license. This Act provided the Government with power to constitute National Parks, Tiger reserves and Bio-spheric reserves all over the country.

Towards 1970s, after a long gap of time, the Government of India was disillusioned by large scale conversion of forest land for various development purposes and rapid reduction in forest cover. With a view to remove the loopholes in the existing provisions of forest laws and to check the dwindling of forest cover due to irrational utilisation of forest lands for non-forest purpose the Government of India introduced the Forest Conservation Act,1980. This Act, thus, have the following major objectives– (a) to check deforestation, (b) to check or rationalise diversion of forest land for non-forest purposes, and (c) to compensate the forest loss, through afforestation in lieu of any forested land diverted. The Forest Conservation Act, 1980 gives direction to the state governments and other authorities not to convert any forested land or any part thereof for any other non-forest purposes without prior approval of the Central Government. In this way the Central Government enters into the affairs of the state government making 'Forest' (so long under state-list) a concurrent subject. The Section 2 of the Act runs as follows:

Notwithstanding anything contained in any other laws in force in the state, no state government or other authority shall make, except with the prior authority of the Central Government, any order directing—

(1) That any reserved forest or any portion thereof shall cease to be reserved.
(2) That any forest land or any portion thereof may be used for non-forest purposes.

(3) That any forest land or portion thereof may be assigned by way of lease or otherwise to any private person or to any authority, corporation, agency or any other organisation not owned by government.

(4) That any forest land may be cleared of trees which have grown naturally in that land for the purpose of using it for re-afforestation.

The expression 'non-forest purposes' mentioned above has been clarified in this Act by stating that it means the cultivation of tea, coffee, spices, rubber, palms, horticulture crops and medicinal plants.

The Act of 1988 barred the leasing out of forest land or any portion of the forest to any individual agency or corporation not owned, managed or controlled by the government. There is also a prohibition towards the plantation of horticultural crops or medicinal plants and shifting cultivation etc. as they constitute non-forest activity. It transpires that the Forest Act 1988 is clearly against the interest of tribals as the above activities are traditionally and exclusively of the tribal people who are a part and parcel of the forest and dependent on forest economy.

National Forest Policy (December, 1988)

Over the past three decades and ever since the launching of the National Forest Policy,1952 the country's forest resources suffered severe depletion due to relentless pressure arising from ever increasing demand for timber, fuelwood, fodder and other forest produces together with inadequacy of effective protective measures, diversion of forest lands for non-forest purposes without ensuring compensatory afforestation. The government attitude towards forest as a source of revenue and means of economic development and lack of public awareness about the value of forest also played a role in the destruction of the forest. There was, therefore, a need to review the whole situation and to evolve a new strategy for protection, conservation and augmentation of the forest wealth of the country. Towards the beginning of the Eighth Five Year Plan, the Government of India adopted a new Forest Forest Policy 1988, with a view to give a new direction and vision to country's forest development. The following are the basic objectives of the Policy.

Basic objectives

- Maintenance of environmental stability through preservation and, where necessary, restoration of the ecological balance that has been adversely disturbed by serious depletion of the forests of the country.
- Natural forests with the vast variety of flora and fauna, which represent the remarkable biological diversity and genetic resources of the country.
- Checking soil erosion and denudation in the catchment areas of rivers, lakes, reservoirs in the "interest of soil and water conservation, for mitigating floods and droughts and for the retardation of siltation of reservoirs.
- Checking the extension of sand-dunes in the desert areas of Rajasthan and along the coastal tracts.
- Increasing substantially the forest/tree cover in the country through massive afforestation and social forestry programmes, especially on all denuded, degraded and unproductive lands.
- Meeting the requirements of fuelwood, fodder, minor forest produce and small timber of the rural and tribal populations.
- Increasing the productivity of forests to meet essential national needs.
- Encouraging efficient utilisation of forest produce and maximising substitution of wood.
- Creating a massive people's movement with the involvement of women, for achieving these objectives and to minimise pressure on existing forests.

The policy emphasised on the maintenance of environmental stability and restoration of the ecological balance through massive afforestation and social forestry programmes. As regards shifting cultivation government should discourage such practices and alternative avenues of income suitably harmonised with right land use practice should be encouraged. The policy also recommended increased activities on forest research and education in Agricultural Universities and other academic institutions and their curriculars and courses for imparting education should updated.

The policy envisaged the need for creating massive people's movement through active involvement of village communities living close to the forest, in protection and development of forest. Pursuant to this policy, the Government of India issued notification to all state governments to involve local communities in the management and protection of forests. This has led to the development of Joint Forest Management (JFM) programmes and a new drive with the help of various NGOs for creating people's awareness on protection of environment. Other areas identified by the National Policy are:

1. Non-regularisation of encroachments.
2. Deploying improved modern forest management practices to deal with forest fires.
3. Increase in forest extension activities.
4. Emphasis on forest education and research activities.

The National Forest Policy, 1988 also aims at having a minimum of one-third of Geographic area of the country under forest cover and enjoin two-thirds of the area under forest in all hill areas.

Forest Cover in the Country

The term 'Forest Cover' includes all lands more than one hectare area having tree canopy density of 10 per cent and above. The basic data for forest cover is obtained from the remote sensing satellite whose sensor captures reflectance of sun light from the tree canopy in multiple bands. In such data, with present technique and skills, no distinction with respect to the trees species has been attempted. Thus, all species of trees (including bamboos, fruits or palms, etc.) and all types of lands (forest, private, community or institutional) satisfying the basic criteria of canopy density of more than 10 per cent have been delineated as forest cover while interpreting satellite data.

According to the 2001 FSR Report the total forest cover of India was 675,538 sq.km and this constituted 20.55 per cent of the geographic area of the country. Of this, 416,809 sq.km or 12.68 per cent is dense forest cover while 258,729 sq. km is open forest cover. The term 'non–forest', on the other hand, includes scrub estimated to cover an area of 47,318 sq. The Table 4.4 gives us, at a glance, the position of our country's forest and vegetation coverage.

Table 4.4 Forest cover in the country

Class	*Area (km²)*	*Per cent of Geographic Area*
Forest Cover		
(a) Dense	416,809	12.68
(b) Open	258,729	7.87
Total Forest Cover	675,538	20.55
Non - forest		
Scrub	47,318	1.44
Total Non – forest	2,611,725	79.45
Total Geographic Area	**3,287,263**	**100.00**

Forest Cover in Meghalaya

The State of Meghalaya has a total geographical area of 22,429 sq. km.of which nearly two-thirds of the area is composed of hills and gorges, thickly covered with forests, shrubs and grasslands. Approximately 69.48 per cent of the total area or 15,584 sq. km. of the geographical area is under forest cover. Out of this, 5,681 sq. km. is covered with dense forest and 9,903 sq. km. is open forest. The forest research scholars and the botanists have found many varieties of trees and groves in Meghalaya which can be broadly grouped under the following heads.

Tropical Forests

These forests are found in the areas up to an elevation of 1200 metre and with an average rainfall of about 100–250 cm. There are numerous sub-types within this category, such as evergreen, semi-evergreen, moist and dry deciduous forests etc. The Tropical evergreen forest is confined to upper reaches of hill range beginning from Tura range extended up to Siju Forest reserved. These forests usually occur in high rainfall areas as well as near catchment areas. They harbour a very rich species diversity where nature is at its extravaganza forming a closed evergreen canopy. Though these forests are not completely free from human interference due to *jhum* practice and seldom form continuous belts, yet the species available here are mighty and often blanketed by lush growth of tropical flora.

The *Tropical semi-evergreen forests* occupy the north eastern and northern slopes of the state, typically up to elevations of 1200 m., where annual rainfall is 150–200 cm. with a comparatively cooler winter. The number of species here are fewer than the evergreen zone. The areas of Ṣaipung and Narpuh reserved forests fall under this category. The dominant trees in these forests are mostly deciduous species, (Sarma, 2003:166) such as *Careya arborea*, *Dillenia pentagyna* and *Callicarpa arborea*.

The *Tropical moist* and *dry deciduous forests* occurs where annual rainfall is below 150 cm and at comparatively low elevations. Typical natural deciduous forests do not occur anywhere in Meghalaya but are only sub–climax or man–made forests. These forests are characterised by seasonal leaf shedding and profuse flowering of the trees. Recurrent forest fires are a common phenomenon here. Deciduous forests are much more extensive in their distribution in the state and include a host of economically important trees like *Shorea robusta*, *Tectona grandis*, *Artocarpus chaplasha* etc. These types of forests are prevalent at lower elevations in Garo Hills, lower Khasi and Jaintia Hills under hot and humid climatic condition. Apart from mixed deciduous forests there are bamboo intruded deciduous forests where a good number of bamboos grow. Bamboo forests are not natural but appear in *jhum* fallows of 15–20 years. These forests at places form pure stands. The common bamboo species in Meghalaya are *Dendrocalamus hamiltonii D. gigantea*, *Bambusa bambos*, *Cephalóstachyum latifolium*, *Chimonobambusa khasiana*, *Melocanna banbusoides* etc. Bamboos also appear in comparatively older forests where there are some gaps in the canopy.

Grasslands and Savanas

Lush green grasslands covering large areas can be seen throughout the Shillong plateau, around Riangdo, Ranikor, Weiloi, Mawphlang, Mawsynram, Cherrapunji, Shillong-Jowai, Jarain and Sutnga in Khasi and Jaintia Hills and major parts of West Garo Hills. Apart from giving a green look to these barren hills, these grasslands also support other dicotyledonous species.

Sub-tropical Pine Forests

The pine forests in Meghalaya are confined to higher reaches of the Shillong plateau in Khasi and Jaintia Hills, in a narrow belt showing an east-west direction. *Pinus kesiya* is the principal species, often forming pure strands. Pine forests of Meghalaya are however not a climax type, but are of secondary nature and is in a stage of succession termination (Haridasan *et al.*, 1985: 18).

Sal Forest

These forests occupy the northern part of Khasi Hills with pure varieties growing in certain parts of Garo Hills. The Rongrengiri Reserve forest is considered to be the best Sal reserve in India . Bamboo forests grow within Sal forests. The wood from Sal (*Shorea robusta*) is generally used for the construction of furniture, railway tract and sleepers, etc.

Classification of forest types in any terrain is such as directly related to environmental factors such as climate, physiography and edaphic (soil). These three factors play a vital role in the growth of particular species of trees and plant vegetation. For example, the climatic elements of temperature, rainfall, relative humidity, etc. could be favourable to a particular plant growth over a considerable period. In the Central and Eastern upland of Meghalaya, sub-tropical moist hill (pine) type of forests is predominant and the dominant tree is pine (*Pinus kesiya*) .

Judicial Intervention

For the first time in the history of Indian forestry the judicial authority of India happened to intervene into the affairs of the forest administration. The Supreme Court involvement in forest conservation matters originated in a Public Interest Litigation (PIL) case – viz, *TN Godavarman* vs. *Union of India* in which the Supreme Court prohibited felling of trees in all forests irrespective of whether they belong to Government or private individuals, except in accordance with the working plan of the state governments which are approved by the Central Government. The Supreme Court re-defined the term "forest" which implies all forests irrespective of their nature, ownership and classification. Prior to this order, the term forest covered only government forests whether they possess any tree or not, while a large areas of lands well covered with trees were not considered as forests in the Forest Conservation Act, 1980. Because of this wrong definition of forest, vast areas of forested lands belonging to individuals and non-government institutions did not come under the purview of Forest Acts and Regulations. This resulted in unrestricted felling of trees and denudation of non-government forests. The State of Meghalaya is one of the hill states where the largest area of forested land is under the ownership of communities, clans and private individuals. According to an estimate, out of the total of 15,584 sq. km of forested area of the state at least 5254 sq. km of forest or nearly one-third of the total forest area belongs to clans and private individuals over which neither the Government of Meghalaya nor the Autonomous District Councils have any control. The owners of these forest lands have their own organisation by the name Meghalaya Forest Land Owners Association to protect their rights and interests and till before the Supreme Court Order of December 12, 1996, putting blanket ban on felling of trees and transporting timber outside the state, they were freely prospecting timbers in their forests disregard of restrictions put against it by the state Forest Department.

Notes

1. Gadgil and Guha, 1992 op. cit. p-
2. *Ibid*, 1992, p-18.
3. CSE, 1982.
4. Kumar, 1992, p-63.
5. Choube. S.K., *Hill Politics in NE*, 1973, p-100-101.
6. Kyndiah, P.R., Rev. Nichols Roy: Architect of District Council Autonomy, 1993 p-68.
7. Department of Forest and Environment, Government of Meghalaya.

5

Forest Policies and the Socio-economic Impact

Colonial Forest Policy

The rich forests resources naturally grown over the hills and valleys of Khasi and Jaintia Hills were taken over by the British Government for imperial benefit. In order to legitimize their occupation over these forests the government made legislations which gave them legal authority to constitute forested areas into reserved forests and protected forests where the local people were prohibited to enter and remove anything. The colonial forest policy, therefore, was characterized by intensification of imperial control over the forest resources of the country for the benefit of the government. In the words of Gadgil and Guha—"Colonialism's most tangible outcome, some of whose effects persist to this day, is related to its global control of resources"[1] The ultimate objective of the British Forest Policy was to preserve and develop the natural grown forests under the cover of law and to harvest their products, i.e. timber and other products for trade and revenue. England required large quantity of timber for ship building and the good quality of Indian wood like sal, teak etc. suited well for the purpose. The British merchants and the royal navy were interested in Indian timber for their naval requirement and from the latter part of eighteenth century the Indian Forest Department was entertaining repeated requests from the British Admiralty for supply of Madras and Burma teak.[2]

British Forest Policy was primarily oriented towards earning of revenue and to achieve that end the government did not spare any means. In Assam a new Forest Department was opened as early as 1868, and Bengal Forest Rules, 1865 were adopted. In that very year an Assistant Conservator of Forest was appointed who looked after the affairs of forest until 1874 when Mr. Gustav Mann took over as Deputy Conservator of Forest.[3] With this, the areas under the control of Forest Department was rapidly increased. In 1874 the area under reserved forest was only 269 sq. miles which increased to 1983 sq. miles in 1879 and in 1895 it increased to 3716 sq. miles.[4] The government income through forest revenue also increased, corresponding to the increase in reserved forest areas. For example, in 1878-79 the revenue receipt increased from Rs. 1,01,098 to Rs. 4,44,706 in 1894-95.[5]

Besides trading in timber with England and other foreign countries, the government leased out forest coups (mahals) to contractors for local use of timber imposing high royalty, firewood mahals were sold out to lessees who prospected for profit by selling out to local people. Cattle grazing reserves were constituted and grazing taxes were levied on cattle on their head counts, at the rate of two Annas on cows and four Annas on buffaloes. The rates were changed from time to time and by 1911-12 the grazing taxes were raised to four annas for cows and rupee one for buffalo.[6]

Towards the close of the nineteenth century construction of railway network started in Assam. In 1881 the Assam Railway and Trading Company started construction of railway line from Dibrugarh to Sadiya which was extended to Doom Dooma and Makum.[7] In 1894 Tezpur-Balipara Line was opened.[8] For construction of these railway lines sal timber sleepers were used which came from the forests of Kamrup, Goalpara and Garo hills districts. For one kilometer length of railway line required 860 pieces of sleepers of 6″ × 4″ × 6ft. sizes which gives us clear idea as to the number of sal trees felled to meet the requirement.[9] The rich forest resource of Assam which was built up by nature during the past centuries was conveniently exploited by the British Government for its revenue and profit.

Post-Independence Forest Policy

The government changed in 1947; national government took over from the colonial government, but the forest policy did not change.

The Government of India continued to follow more or less the same forest laws. The Indian Forest Act 1927 and the Assam Forest Regulation 1891, the two major forest laws, continued to be applied in whole state of Assam including Khasi and Jaintia Hills district. In 1952 the Government of India declared a new forest policy viz, National Forest Plolicy, 1952, which envisaged—(1) maintenance of environmental stability through preservation and restoration of ecological balance, (2) conserving the natural heritage of the country by preserving the remaining natural forests with the vast variety of flora and fauna, (3) checking soil erosion and denudation in the catchment areas of rivers, lakes and reservoirs, (4) increasing sustainability of forest/tree cover in the country, and (5) meeting the requirement of fuel, fodder, minor forest produce, small timber for the rural and tribal population. But, unfortunately, the government did not come up with new forest laws, to achieve the objectives laid down therein and the high ideals held out by the National Forest Policy remained merely a rhetoric.

In 1952 Autonomous District Councils were constituted in the hill districts of Assam under the Sixth Schedule of the Constitution of India which took up administration and control of forests under their jurisdictions. In the district of Khasi and Jaintia Hills the existing forest areas were bifurcated between the state Forest Department and the Khasi and Jaintia Hills Autonomous District Council. With this division of forests, all reserved forests, government forest, existing parks and gardens remained with the state Forest Department, while the rest of the forest areas of the district went under the management of the District Council. The Khasi and Jaintia Hills Autonomous District Council promulgated its own Forest Act under the title "United Khasi and Jaintia Hills Autonomous District (Management and Control of Forest) Act, 1958 but the objectives of the Act remained, more or less, dittoed the previous Acts. It classified the forests under the District Council as, Protected forests, Unclassed forests, Village forests and Private forests and sought to control and manage them with the meagre fund allocation received from the Centre and State Government. The forest areas that came under jurisdiction of the District Council being larger than it could manage with its small Forest staff they became merely a source of revenue earning. The Protected forests, the legacy from the state Forest Department, being rich in timber value, were exploited it to the point of its denudation by the District Council.

After the State of Meghalaya was carved out of Assam in 1972, the state Legislative Assembly adopted the Assam Forest Regulation 1891, under the title Meghalaya Forest Regulation (Application and Amendment) Act, 1973. This Act empowers the government to constitute a reserved forest at any land at the disposal of the government in a manner provided therein. But so far no reserved forest could be constituted in Khasi Hills or Jaintia Hills as there was no land at the disposal of the government in these districts. It also deals with constitution of Village Forests and to frame rules related to it. Thus, it is seen that the existing forest laws enacted by the colonial rulers are merely adopted and continued to be followed by the government without any change in the basic policy or in the pattern of forest administration. Neither the State Government nor the District Council showed any intention to preserve and protect forest for the sake of environment and ecological balance and for future generation.

Forest for Development

With the implementation of a series of Five Year Plans by the Government of India since 1952 onwards, the nation got into rapid strides along the path of progress and development. There was rapid growth in agriculture, industries, health and sanitation, literacy and education etc. leading to socio-economic development and better standard of living of the community. The government aimed at harnessing all the resources of the country for all round economic development. The forest was found to be one of the potential natural resources for industrial and infrastructural development. Timbers were liberally used in construction of buildings, bridges, furniture and other structures. Forest based small and cottage industries like saw mill, veneer mill, carpentry workshop, etc. grew up all over the country pushing up the demand for various qualities of wood. Large scale bamboo groves were denuded to meet the demand of paper-pulp for burgeoning paper mills. Thus, there was a paradigm shift in the basic Forest Policy of the government from the colonial 'forest for revenue' to the national 'forest for development', both being equally destructive of the forest resources and detrimental to the people who live in close communion with nature. The high ideals held out by the National Forest Policy were flouted away; every possible element of the forest was harnessed in development activities; pristine forest wealth was exploited resulting in large scale destruction of forest cover. To cite a concrete example, the FSL, in monitoring the forest cover of Meghalaya on a two-year cycle found that the total forest cover of 15,633 sq. km in 1999 was reduced to 15,584sq. km in 2001, showing a net loss of 49 sq. km.[10] The following paragraphs will give us an account of the impact that have been made upon the social and economic life of the common people due to destruction and alienation of forest from them.

Socio-economic Impact

Before the advent of the British the people of the North East had very little need of the forest resources. In the hill districts the Khasis and other tribals lived peacefully in perfect harmony with forest. The forest was a well loved home which they never exploited for their profit except for their home consumption, instead they preserved it as store-house of their livelihood. They believed the forests as the sacred abodes of gods and spirits and looked at them with a sense of reverence and awe and never dared to disturb the sanctum-sanctorum of the place. They took away from the forest what is barely needed for their livelihood and let the flora and fauna to grow and flourish in their solitary habitats. This was true, more or less, of all the tribal societies of the North East.

The colonial forest policy was, therefore, a first assault on the traditional life of the tribal people of the North East in general and the Khasis and Jaintias in particular. There were, primarily, three colonial Forest Acts which had decisive impact on the socio-cultural and economic profiles of the tribals-Indian Forest Act VII of 1865, Indian Forest Act of 1878 and the Forest Act of 1927. The first Act of 1865 declared certain forest areas as Protected forests and excluded the people from their benefits; the second Act of 1878 came as a more concrete law which conferred the government with the right to constitute Reserved Forests on 'any forest land or waste land which is the property of the government' This Act not only debarred the local people from entering into and removing any forest produce from the reserved forest and protected forests but also permanently alienated them from the land itself. This had a far reaching affect on the livelihood of the people in more than one way. Firstly, agriculture being the main stay of the people, the land constitutes primary factor of their economy. Secondly, and more significantly, land, for the hill people who grow their food by jhum cultivation, means a natural resource available in abundance for shifting cultivation changing from place to place. The Khasis carry out jhum or shifting cultivation which is locally called '*Thang Shyrti*'. It is a forest based method of cultivation followed by them since time immemorial. This type of cultivation, despite its many demerits and adverse opinions, has come to stay in Khasi society even to this day. This is, mainly because of their peculiar land tenure system. The land tenure system in Khasi and Jaintia Hills recognizes two types of land—*Ri-Raid* or community land and *Ri-Kynti* or private land. Every member of the community has the right to carry out cultivation anywhere on the community land, at his will and free of cost, as long as he wants. In case, he abandons the land for a consecutive period of three years and shifts to some other land, the land occupied by him will revert back to the community and becomes Ri-Raid land. A community with this system of social economy was, therefore, affected more than anybody else, by the British Forest Policy which appropriated their land of jhum cultivation.

The land and the forest, the two most crucial factors of village economy over which the people enjoyed irreversible rights were increasingly appropriated by the British Government as the demand for timber increased. The proprietary rights, thus, established by the colonial rulers through promulgation of laws, permanently deprived the people of their traditional rights. The following extract from Indian Forest Act VII of 1878, cleverly crafted to suit the colonial interest, clearly reflects the commercial intention of the government.[11] It runs— "The local government may, from time to time constitute any forest land or waste land which is the property of the government or over which the government has proprietary rights or to the whole or part of forest produce of which the government is entitled, a reserved forest"[12]. Needless to say, "the British Rule in India, like other western empires elsewhere in the developing world could be regarded as an elaborate system of resource extraction and allocation, determining who was to have access to nature's wealth."[13]

In Assam the colonial government attached more importance to agriculture than to forest by bringing more land under tillage in order to augment income through land revenue. As a result, large areas of forest land were reclaimed and brought under cultivation. People of Nepalese origin were encouraged to come to Assam even providing them onward journey expenses.[14] They were liberally given settlement of waste lands which resulted in large scale destruction and denudation of forests. The land area occupied by Nepali cultivators rapidly ncreased from 17000 acres in 1913-14 to 28000 in 1919-20.[15] By the year 1939-40 the total land area occupied and cultivated by Nepalese rose to 104773 acres.[16] This policy of the government for bringing more land under agriculture resulted in steep reduction of the forest cover of Assam.

Towards the middle of nineteenth century tea industry received special attention of the Government in Assam. A number of British Tea Companies were set-up for which the government incorporated legal provision named 'special cultivation' in the Assam Land and Revenue Regulation and gave liberal settlement of large areas of waste land to Tea Companies for tea cultivation at nominal prices. For this purpose the government introduced West Land Grant Rules of 1838, Fee Simple Rules of 1826, Revised Fee Simple RUles of 1874 and the New Lease Rules of 1876. Under the cover of these rules vast areas of waste lands of Assam, even more than actual requirement, were leased out to tea gardens under liberal terms of 99 years lease. As per Annual Tea Report for 1878 the total area of waste land granted to tea gardens of Assam under the Waste Land Grant Rules of 1838, stood at 5,87,409 acres, which includes 2,071 acres from Khasi and Jaintia Hills.[17] By the year 1920s a large number of tea gardens were established in various districts of Assam particularly in upper Assam and the northern banks of mid Assam valley. This resulted in reclamation and conversion of more areas of jungles and forest into tea gardens. The scarcity of labour for working in the tea gardens induced the tea companies to import labourers from Bihar, Orissa, Central Province, etc. By 1931, the population of those migrant labourers went up to 1.3 million, which was one-sixth of the total population of Assam itself.[18] In course of time these immigrant tea garden labourers started to live in Assam permanently in the new Busties that grew up around tea gardens and merged with general population of the province.

The Nepali cattle rearers preferred hill areas for their occupation of milk production because of climatic and topographical factors which are similar to their own country of Nepal. They came to the hill districts of Assam like, Naga Hills, Lushai Hills Manipur, Khasi and Jaintia Hills, Garo Hills, etc. and started milk supply business. The retired Gorkha soldiers were encouraged by the government to settle up in the places of their posting who also took up cattle rearing and cultivation. According to an official record the cattle rearing by Nepalis goes back to 1892 when the number of tax paying cows was 462 for which grazing tax amounting to Rs. 6,772 was realized. As the number of immigrant Nepalis increased in Assam the revenue on account of grazing tax rose from Rs. 1,83,000 in 1916-17 to Rs. 3,41,000 in 1920-21. The business of producing milk and milk products became monopoly of the Nepalis in the North East. In fact, it was the Nepalis who commercialized milk production in Assam and first started the use of milk in tea in the hill districts. The grazing tax, kept on rising from Rs. 1,83,000 in 1916-17 to Rs. 3,41,000 in 1920-21, and soon became a major source of revenue for the government. The number of cattle also increased from 42000 in 1915-16 to 86325 in 1920-21.[19] This had adverse affect upon the natural growth of forest vegetation, on the one hand, and caused damage of crops grown by the cultivators. Complaints from the public about the destruction of crops by the cattle of Nepali Bathans were frequently heard in Khasi and Jaintia Hills and also in Naga hills. The government was well aware of it but remained indifferent and inactive as long as it obtained handsome revenue.

The tribals in the North East, on more than one occasion, expressed their resentment and protest against the government policy of alienating them from their well loved forest and primary source of livelihood. The history goes back to the British Rule when the Garos rose in revolt against the conversion of their jhum lands into reserved forests and restricting them from entering and using the land. The most immediate consequence of the Indian Forest Act of 1878 was visible in the discontentment of the forest communities who now totally lost control over their own habitats. The Forest Act of 1878 evolved a sharp reaction from the simple and straight-forward Garo community who rose in popular revolt in an attempt to restore their traditional rights to freely roam about their forest habitats. The government, however, arrested their leader one Sonaram Sangma and imprisoned him for a short time. This led the Garos to file a public petition on 9th February, 1906 signed by more than one lakh Garos to Lord Minto, the Viceroy and Governor General of India. The petition accused the government stating that their ancestors had enjoyed the privilege of living in the forest in Garo Hills, made use of the forest products, sold them for their benefit besides cultivating their land and having the rights of pasturage, but the government has deprived them of this age old privileges.[20] Nothing, however was done by the colonial government towards the redressal of their grievance.

As the implementation of Five Year Plans progressed in the country, more lands were required for multifarious development purposes. Large areas of land were utilized for construction of a network of roads and communication, establishment of institutional buildings, extension of townships, industrial sites, stadiums and airports etc. These lands were, undoubtedly, acquired by government at the cost of either agriculture or forest lands. The construction of irrigation canals, dams and reservoirs for hydro-electricity uprooted many families from their hearths and homes. In Khasi Hills an area of 4000 acres of cultivated and home-stead land was submerged under reservoir for hydro-electricity by constructing a dam across Umiam river. In Garo Hills an area of several thousand hectares of land has been acquired by government for setting up a Bio-sphere Reserve. A new Air Port was established in Garo Hills and the existing Air-field at Umroi, in Khasi Hills was upgraded by acquisition of large areas of land. These hill areas, before they were acquired by government, were forested land used by villagers for jhum cultivation. It is, thus evident that a considerable chunk of agriculture and forest land was diverted by government in the name of national development programmes which contributed to severe impact on the socio-economic condition of the people who depended on the land for their subsistence.

The Government of India passed Wild Life (Protection) Act, in 1972 which was a step forward towards the strengthening of conservation of flora and fauna of the country. Long ago, during the

British Rule one such legislation existed by the title Wild Birds and Animals Protection Act, 1912. The new Act passed by the Government of India provided much needed security to the birds and animals, many of which were in the verge of extinction, but at the same time it went directly against the interest of the common people by diversion of more lands for extension/creation of Wild-life Sanctuaries, National Parks, Tiger Reserves, etc.

The Forest Conservation Act, 1980 was considered as a significant piece of legislation insofar as it sought to ban irrationale conversion of forest lands to non-forest purposes, as we have seen large scale conversion in the foregoing paragraphs. It also aimed at imposition of compensatory afforestation in lieu of forested land diverted on unavoidable circumstances. Undoubtedly, this was a step in the right direction which sought to provide legal protection to dwindling forest. This Act, however, was not subservient to the needs of the people as it infringed the traditional rights of the tribals by restraining them from using their community lands for jhum cultivation, which is traditionally done in forested land. It also restricts them from cultivating tea, coffee, spices, rubber, and horticultural crops. Bacause the Act defines these crops as 'non-forest crops' and bans cultivating on any forest land. These are the crops which grow well in the hill areas, because of climate and hilly terrain, and primarily the hill people cultivate them. It will, thus, be seen that the tribal people living in the hills, like Khasis, Garos, Nagas, Mizos, etc. are gradually being marginalized by the government through bringing in various forest laws. The Government of India seemed to be more conscious about the degradation of forests rather than being concerned about the livelihood of the people who traditionally depend on it. For, no forest law so far enacted by government provides for the safeguard of the rights and interest of the people who are the real protectors of forest.

The Government of India declared a revised *National Forest Policy 1988* with the view to increasing, substantially, the forest cover in the country and to maintain the environmental stability. One of the significant objectives of the policy was to meet the requirement of fuel, fodder, minor forest produce and small timber for the rural tribal population. In order to implement this policy the Ministry of Forest and Environment, in June 1990 issued a circular to all Forest Departments of states to launch *Joint Forest Management (JFM)* programme for revival, restoration and development of degraded forests along with participation of the people. A number of states including Meghalaya followed the instruction of Central Government and started the JFM programme in various districts. The programme has achieved some degree of success in building up non-timber forest resources in the most degraded forests adopted by the Forest Management Committees. The Forest Management Committees involve all the households in the village as members of its general body of the Committee, where the decisions are jointly taken and afforestation activities are done with their collective labour. The Joint Forest Management (JFM) programme, however, could not mitigate the people's livelihood problems arising out of the loss of their forest habitats. The prolonged application of development oriented government policy in the realm of natural resource management resulted in inevitable impact on the forest community whose livelihood depended on forest. Thus, the larger section of the people living in the rural areas continued to be marginalized by the forest policy and administration adopted by government.

The greatest impact on the livelihood of the forest community was made by the Supreme Court order of 12th December, 1996 imposing complete ban on felling trees from any forest, irrespective of ownership and doing trade in timber. The Apex Court intervention in forest operation originated from a PIL case, viz. *TN Godavarman* vs. *Union Government of India*, 1995 in which the Supreme Court suspended felling of trees in all forests irrespective of whether it belonged to government or any private person, except in accordance with the working plans of the state government formally approved by the Central Government. The Supreme Court also interpreted the term 'Forest' as all forested lands disregard of their classification and nature of ownership. Prior to this order, the term forest implied only the government forest whether it covered any tree or not, while lands with significant cover of tree were not regarded as forests and the people were free to cut down trees from anywhere grown in their lands. Because of this lacunae in the definition of forest, large areas of forest belonging to private owners did not fall within the purview of the Forest Conservation Act, 1980 and they were being severely deforested by their owners without any restriction. In Khasi and Jaintia Hills, unlike any other parts of India, great majority of forests belong to community/clans and private individuals on which the state Forest Department or the Autonomous District Councils have no control. Nearly one-third of the total forest area of Meghalaya is owned by community/clan or private individuals. Before the Supreme Court Order, 1996, these proprietors of private forests caused large scale felling of trees from their forests to make quick bucks which led to near denudation of forests.

The Supreme Court Order, 1996 not only brought about a grinding halt on the felling of trees heralding a new era of security to flora and fauna, but also had a far reaching impact on the livelihood of a large section of the working class people engaged in the forest industry. The impact was felt more severely in the hill areas of Khasi and Jaintia Hills where the tribal economy was traditionally based on forest. A large community of people beginning from those who worked in the forest operation and transport of logs to those who were engaged in saw mills, vinneer mills, factories, carpentry workshops and building of houses etc. were virtually thrown out of employment as a result of this judicial activism. The Supreme Court Order banned forest operation but did not order for providing alternative source of income to those who lost their jobs. In fact, the entire natural resource management policy of the government lacked livelihood focus for those who depend on forest. There was also lack of community involvement in policy process. Many issues primarily concerning common man and their livelihood related issues do not get reflected in the government policies.

A survey was conducted by the Department of Botany, North East Hill University, under the guidance of Prof. S.K. Barik and V.T. Darlong to study the impact of government resource management policy on the livelihood of forest poor. They took up nine villages in five districts of Meghalaya for this study. It was found that in all the nine villages forest dependence was high due to the practice of shifting cultivation, timber trade and NTFP (Non-Timber Forest Produce) collection. In one particular village named Mawthoh of West Khasi Hills district, they found that there were 20 households with 150 persons. 63 per cent of the village area was under forest which were entirely owned by private individuals, 31 per cent was agricultural land and 6 per cent was kitchen garden. All the households were dependent on forest for their livelihood. After the Supreme Court

Order 1996, a few families turned to charcoal making, some other to agriculture and kitchen gardening. Before the Supreme Court Order, income of the village from forest timber business was Rs. one lakh per year which came down to zero as a result of the judicial order. Due to impact of the Supreme Court order the income from agriculture increased to Rs. 40,000, from kitchen garden Rs. 10,000 and from mining labour to Rs. 20,000 per year. Some of the families shifted to charcoal making, bee-keeping, etc.

In the following chapters we shall further examine and assess the emerging trend in the Khasi economy due to changes in forest policy and administration in Khasi and Jaintia Hills.

Notes

1. Gadgil, Madhav and Guha, Ramchandra, *The Fissured Land: An Ecological History of India*, p. 116.
2. *Ibid.*, p. 119.
3. Goswami, S.D., *Aspects of Revenue Administration in Assam*, p. 119.
4. Handique, R., *British Forest Policy in Assam*, p. 74.
5. *Ibid.*, p. 99.
6. Bryant F. Beadas, *A Note of Inspection of Some Forests of Assam*, p. 6.
7. Medhi, S.B., *Transport System and Economic Development in Assam*, p. 67.
8. *Ibid.*, p. 85-86.
9. Gadgil, Guha, *op. cit.* p. 122.
10. Shangpliang. Rekha, *Forest in the Life of the Khasis*, 2010, p. 21.
11. Kannan. K.P., Forest For Industry's Profit, *in Economic and Political Weekly*, June 5, 1982.
12. Indian Forest Act, 1878, Published by Government of India Press.
13. Tuker, Richard P., The Depletion of India's Forest under British Imperialism: Planters, Foresters and Peasants in Assam and Kerela, in Worster (ed) *Ends of Earth*, p. 118.
14. Borpujari, H.K. (ed) *Political History of Assam*, Vol. V, p. 48.
15. Report on the Land Revenue Administration of Assam, 1919-20.
16. Report on Land Revenue Administration of Assam Valley Division, 1939-40.
17. Brandis, D., *Suggestions Regarding Forest Administration in Assam*, p. 7.
18. Borpujari, H.K., *Comprehensive History of Assam*, Vol. V.

19. Gurung, Tejimala, Human Movement and the Colonial State: the Nepalis of the North East India British Empire, in *Nepalis in North East India* (ed) A.C. Sinha and T.B. Subba, 2003.
20. Sinha, A.C., 1993 *Beyond the Trees, Tigers: Historical Sociology of the Eastern Himalayan Forests*, p. 115.

6

Profile of Lawbyrwa Villa

Location

Lawbyrwa village is located in the Ri Bhoi District of Meghalaya under Umsning Development Block and falls within Mylliem Syiemship. It lies to the north of Shillong, the state capital of Meghalaya, at a distance of 22.kms from Shillong. The village can be reached by a motorable metalled road and is well connected to the Guwahati-Shillong highway.

Lawbyrwa, as a composite whole, is a large village which is composed of three distinct Blocks namely:

1. Lawbyrwa No. 5
2. Proper Byrwa village
3. Lawbyrwa No. 4

The two Blocks Lawbyrwa Nos. 4 and 5 are located on either sides of the proper Byrwa village and form a part of the main village in the sense that the three share the same infrastructural settings and fall under one village administration called *Durbar Shnong*. There are four adjoining villages surrounding Lawbyrwa. Towards the East lies Law Pyllun village, which is approximately 4 kms eastward. To the West lies Umtring village, which is about 3 kms westward. To the North lies Umthan village approximately 3 kms away and to the South lies Byrwa village, which is 5 kms away from Lawbyrwa. The total geographical area of the village is approximately 15 sq kms. The population distribution in the village is shown with the help of Table 6.1.

Table 6. 1: Population Distribution of Lawbyrwa Village

	Male	*Female*	*Total*
Adult	163	141	304
Minor	181	170	351
Total	**344**	**311**	**655**

Source: Block Office Umsning Block

The population figures show a total population of 655 members including both adult and minors. There has not been a sudden rise or fall in the population figure of the village as per village records but on interview with older members of the village, it was revealed that a serious plague (*khlam*) had once hit the village many years ago which affected the inhabitants who had to flee to the outskirts of the village. This must have been one of the reasons for the low population density in the village.

Land and Geography

The village Lawbyrwa as a component of the greater Ri-Bhoi region falls within sub-montane territory and is characterised by undulating hills running north and south which seldom attain the heights above 600 metres. It has a moderate slope from 5° to 10° angle gradually sliding down towards Brahmaputra valley (Sarma, 2003). The study of the inclination of land surface is significant in order to understand the development of soil, loss of soil due to weathering, mining operation and agricultural practice like *Jhum* cultivation. The National Bureau of Soil Survey (NBSS) and Land Use Planning (LUP) of Jorhat, Assam conducted a detailed study of Meghalaya soil condition and classified it into four social orders, 8 sub-orders and 14 soil groups. According to this soil classification, the entire Ri-Bhoi belt including village Lawbyrwa has predominantly laterite order of soil. The soil is yellowish red in colour and poor in nutrients and acidic in reaction. This is due to weathering of rocks like granite, quartzite, schist, gneisses and conglomerates, etc. (Sarma, 2003).

The River System

Lawbyrwa has two important rivers flowing through it which discharge their waters into the river Brahmaputra. They are (1) Wah-Um-Trew, and (2) Wah-Um-Sumer. The former takes its rise from the legendary 'Sohpetbneng' hill and turns to the westerly course, crossing the Shillong-Guwahati Highway and after reaching the plain of Assam takes the name of Digaru and ultimately flows into Brahmaputra. The Wah-Um-Trew is known for the water being first harnessed for electric power generation at Byrnihat during Assam Government. A third important river that contributed to power generation is the river Um-ïam which though does not literally flow through the village Lawbyrwa yet has a great bearing with this village. A dam has been constructed into the river Um-Trew and to create an artificial lake at Barapani, which is hardly 2 kms away from Lawbyrwa. From this reservoir water is taken to the Hydro-Electric Power House located at Lawbyrwa for generation of electricity.

Rainfall

Monsoon rains seasonally feed the village abundantly. There is no rain-gauge installation at the village but according to rainfall recorded at Umling located at a distance of 5 kms from the village, the average annual rainfall is 2146 mm this may be considered as moderate. Shillong, the capital of Meghalaya, located in the rain shadow region of Central Plateau receives 2359 mm annually, which is almost equal with Lawbyrwa. The monsoon season normally starts from May and continues till September. The monsoon days are congenial to farmers providing agro-climatic conditions favourable for wet cultivation. The winter is dry with about 20 mm of rainfall in average.

Forest and Vegetation

The vegetation of Khasi Hills can be broadly classified into two major types: (1) Tropical, and (2) Warm Temperate type. The tropical type of vegetation cover areas up to an elevation of about 990 metres (Simon, 1991). Lawbyrwa falls under tropical vegetation type and has mostly evergreen and semi-evergreen forest and grasslands. Most of the forested areas are dominated by Khasi-Pine (*Pinus kasiya*) while many other varieties of wild fruit bearing trees, shrubs and thatch are grown profusely. Bamboo thickets of different types and wild banana trees cover the hill slopes.

Land Ownership and Land-use Pattern

The concept of land as property is central to the forest based economy of Lawbyrwa village. Though land is primarily a natural resource, it ensures economic security to the villagers and above all in Khasi Hills where most of the lands are held by common property by the clans it plays an important role in strengthening ties within that clan.

As is evident in other parts of the country, the impact of social change and the need for development have gradually eroded the tribal rights over their land and have brought significant changes in the pattern of land distribution and land use. The village under study, Lawbyrwa is not an exception to this observation. In the wake of economic development that obtained in these areas, as early as 1950's, Hydro-electric Project was established around Lawbyrwa village which submerged thousands of acres of cultivated land under water reservoir and considerable areas of land were acquired by the government for construction of roads and buildings. In the process, poor cultivators were dispossessed of their lands and rendered landless. It is learnt from the village elders that many of the landowners were deprived of their legitimate land compensation due to their ignorance about the law.

The fact of land alienation from poor cultivators to richer section of society is a universal feature of Indian rural economy. This fact is equally applicable in respect of village Lawbyrwa and for that matter for the whole of Ri-Bhoi district, which is considered as the rice-bowl of Khasi Hills. Studies carried out by various sample surveys have indicated that most of fertile lands in this district are under the possession of well-to-do people of Shillong who have converted them into orchards, pineapple and tea gardens. Other low-lying lands suitable for wet paddy cultivation are rented out to landless farmers. There was emergence of a class of landless cultivators as well as absentee landlords in many parts of Khasi Hills.

In respect of Lawbyrwa village Table 6.2 will illustrate the landownership pattern.

Table 6.2: Land Ownership Pattern

Sl. No.	*Amount of Land (Acres)*	*No. of Households*	*Percentage*
1.	Above 10 acres	6	10
2.	5-10 acres	12	20
3.	Up to 5 acres	30	50
4.	Landless families	12	20
Total		**60**	**100**

Source: Fild work data

Table shows that the land ownership pattern is unevenly distributed. Out of a total of 60 sample households, a large number of 30 households own land upto only 5 acres and only 6 households hold land up to 10 acres. Not many families are landless and neither do many families own lands. Those who do not own lands work on other's land on hire and those who own even a small plot of about 5 acres cultivate it or give it on hire.

Land-use Pattern

The pattern of rural land use is invariably associated with micro-geographical conditions such as topography, climate (humidity conditions) and soil fertility. In the present study of Lawbyrwa village, the analysis of land use data indicates the dominance of land under forest (700 acres). The second important land use category in the village is arable land of which the proportion is greater in the hilly slopes where the villagers practise shifting cultivation. The proportion of land under agricultural use is 300 acres out of a total geographical area of 15 sq kms. It has been found that the settlements along the hills slopes or foothills offer better scope for diversified land use pattern. Only two types of cultivation practices are followed in the village—shifting and settled cultivation. The total area under *jhum* cultivation is 250 acres and the total number of households involved in *jhum* cultivation is 70. The total area under settled cultivation is 50 acres and the number of households involved in settled cultivation is 25. There are a few families who follow both methods of cultivation, which accounts to 20 households. These families carry out settled cultivation in the plains bordering the foothills next to their settlements and *jhum* cultivation is practised on the hill slopes. As has been mentioned before, Lawbyrwa being a deeply forested village, the total land area under forest cover is 700 acres, which is the most dominant feature in the pattern of land use in the village.

The interpretation of land use data becomes more meaningful when we show it in the form of Table 6.3:

Table 6.3: Land Use Pattern

Sl. No.	Pattern of Land Use	Total Area (Acres)	No. of Households
1.	Cultivated Land	300	115
2.	*Jhum* Cultivation	250	70
3.	Settled Cultivation	50	25
4.	Horticulture	0	—
5.	Forested	700	—

Source: Fieldwork Data.

Infrastructure

Basic infrastructural facilities like electricity, water supply, health, education and others are directly related to the degree of development of an area. In Lawbyrwa village development is still a far cry, although the village falls under the Umsning Development Block and is entitled to schemes from the Government, not much has been achieved so far. The village still lacks many of the basic infrastructures like hospitals, schools, market, etc.

Health

So far as health care system is concerned the village has no hospital or dispensary. Personal interviews with the respondents revealed that in cases of mild illnesses like common cold, fever, cuts and wounds etc., the villagers had to depend on their own stock of herbal medicines, which they procured before hand and kept them at home. But in many cases, they have to depend on doctors from Shillong by sending someone for the medicines or the patient is directly taken to the city hospitals. Thus, the villagers cannot meet their medical needs, as they still have to travel long distances to be accessible to health care.

Education

It was in 1969 that the Meghalaya State Electricity Board (MSEB) established an MSEB High School in the village. Ever since, it has been an asset to the villagers so much so that the school today has earned a name for itself in respect of the HSLC results, that are fairly good. There is one ME school opened under the SSA (*Shiksha Sabha*) Scheme and one Government LP School.

Government Offices

Situated in the heart of the village is the MSEB Stage-I (4 × 9 Megawatt) Power Station, which has done commendable job in supplying electricity to the entire village besides serving the needs of the State as a whole. Eversince, the Power Station office was set-up, village roads were well constructed and linked to every nook and corner of the village, a High School was set-up and the hillocks are dotted with staff quarters, office buildings, Inspection Bungalow, Central Store House and a Network of black topped motorable road all around the village.

Local Administration

The village has a *Durbar Shnong* (Village Council) headed by a *Tymmen Shnong* or Village headman and assisted by one Assistant Headman who looks after the administrative matters of the village. According to Khasi traditional administrative system a village or a group of few small villages constitute one nucleus administrative unit at the grassroot level. In each such administrative unit there is a *Durbar Shnong* or village council composed of each adult person of the village as members of the *Durbar*. At the higher level there is the *Syiem/Sirdar* with a set of *Myntris* (Ministers) who are responsible for the administration of the *Hima Syiemship* as a whole. They are entrusted with the task of administration of justice, trial of petty cases, control and management of weekly *hats*, road, communication and all other developmental activities of the *Hima Syiemship*. Any appeal against the orders of the *Syiem* or *Sirdar* lies in the District Council Courts. At the District level there is the Autonomous District Council constituted under the 6th Schedule of the Constitution of India and vested with the power of appointment of *Syiem/Sirdar*, management and control of land revenue, forest, primary education, administration of justice and protection and preservation of Khasi culture and tradition.

At the grassroot level the *Durbar Shnong* is the last functionary of the District Council as well as the Government and it carries out overall activities for the development and welfare of the village people. The headman is also empowered to try and dispose petty cases and to look after the law and order of the village and maintain peace and security within the village in times of emergencies. He is the guardian of traditional Khasi custom and good conduct and any member of the society found engaged in illegal trade, immoral act or going against the customary rules can be ex-communicated or even extradited from the village itself. Matters relating to overall well being of the community are sometimes looked after by a *Seng Long Kmie* (Womens' Association), *Seng Samla* (Youth Club) and VLC (Village Level Committee), which are very active in the village.

Forest Profile of Lawbyrwa Village

Traditionally, forest plays an important role in the life of the people of Lawbyrwa village. Forests emerge as the central natural resource governing the basic pattern of livelihood of the people. It provides them with the basic necessities of life such as timber, food, fodder, shelter and medicine. The economic structure of the village itself is built upon the forest where activities like food gathering, hunting, shifting cultivation and selling of forest produces form the basic fulcrum of their economy. The state of the forests is, therefore, an important yardstick for determining the standard and quality of life of the people of this village.

Forest Cover and Vegetation Type of Lawbyrwa Village

Lawbyrwa is one of the well-forested villages of Meghalaya. It has 728.74 hectares of land covered with forest out of its total geographical area of 1200 hectares. Thus, the forest cover in Lawbyrwa accounts to 60.73 per cent of the village area as against 42.37 per cent of forest in Meghalaya.

The forests are mostly of tropical vegetation type with evergreen and semi-evergreen trees and extensive grasslands. The Khasi pine (*Pinus kesiya*) being the dominant tree species of the village, many other varieties of wild fruit bearing trees and tall grass (thatch) are grown profusely which provide the villagers with house-roofing material and plenty of wild fruits from season to season. Large areas of hill slopes and deep gorges are covered with wild grown bamboos, banana trees and innumerable varieties of edible and non-edible mushroom, tubers and succours throughout the year. The tender shoots from the bamboo thickets are a tribal delicacy consumed as a curry or pickle. The dark and green vegetations are the ideal homes to many unknown plants and herbs of great medicinal values in which the Khasis have developed a highly effective lore of traditional system of medicine since time immemorial. Broomstick, which is locally called *"synsar"*, is widely grown in this village and is a good source of income to the people. The village women and children are engaged in collecting broomstick, drying them and selling in bundles to wholesale dealers.

List of Types of Trees and Vegetation Growing in Lawbyrwa

Sl. No.	*Botanical Names*	*Local Names*
1.	*Pinus kesiya*	*Dieng Kseh*
2.	*Shorea robusta*	*Dieng Sal*
3.	*Schima khasiana*	*Dieng Ngan*
4.	*Emblica officianalis*	*Dieng Sohmylleng*
5.	*Musa paradisica*	*Dieng Kait*
6.	*Aegle marmelos*	*Soh Bel*
7.	*Bambusa species*	*Siej*
8.	*Artocarpus heterophylla*	*Sohphan*
9.	*Ficus species*	*Banyan tree*
10.	*Chukrasia tabularis*	*Soh phieng*
11.	*Myrica esculenta*	*Soh phieng*
12.	*Castanopsis species*	*Dieng Soh Od*
13.	*Lantana camarra*	*Dieng Soh Baiongkhlieh*
14.	*Litches species*	*Ding Soh Manir*
15.	*Longifera indica*	*Soh Pieng*
16.	*Dendrocalamus hemiltonii*	*Siej*

Ownership and Management of Forest in Lawbyrwa

On the basis of rights of ownership, management and control, forests in Lawbyrwa are divided into:

(a) Village Forests or *Khlaw Shnong*
(b) Private Forest or *Khlaw Shimet/shikur*.

Village Forest or Khlaw Shnong

Village forests are in existence in almost every Khasi village. A patch of land near the village is earmarked for the purpose of village forest, which symbolises the intimacy that the Khasis have with nature, especially in the use of forest products for their domestic requirements. It also indicates the eco-consciousness and wisdom of the Khasi forefathers who had realised the usefulness of the forest and laid down the system of preserving such forests in every village. In Lawbyrwa, the village forest is preserved, protected and maintained for the benefit of the villagers either collectively on occasions like village festivals, social functions and religious ceremonies, etc. or individually in times of damage of houses by natural calamities or fire accidents etc. The village forest in Lawbyrwa has also served the resource needs of the community through its availability for water catchment facilities and conservation of drinking water for the entire village. It was found through discussion and personal observation that the main water sources for drinking and washing clothes within the village came from the village forest itself.

Management of Village Forest

The control and management of the village forest rests with the Village Durbar, the traditional political institution. The Durbar with the Headman (*Rangbah Shnong*) as the head is responsible for the protection, preservation and development of the village forest. In accordance with this, the Durbar lays down rules and regulations and makes decisions from time to time regarding the use of such forests. Entering into the forest and cutting down trees or shrubs is strictly prohibited and anyone found breaking the rule or violating the norms is punished with fine. So also the water source is protected from misuse or pollution by the village Durbar. The village forest in Lawbyrwa presents quite an impressive sight with a wide variety of vegetational growth of large and medium height growing in size and density thus making it difficult to quantify the exact area and size of such a forest, while some villages in Khasi Hills have more than one village forests, Lawbyrwa has only one, but sufficient enough to cater to the needs of the village community.

Private Forest or Khlaw Shimet/Shikur

Private forests are the forests existing within the private lands (*Ri-Kynti*). On the basis of rights of ownership, these forests can be divided into two: (i) Forest owned by individual owners (*Khlaw shimet*); (ii) Forest owned by a clan (*Khlaw shikur*).

Management of Private Forest

The ownership, control and management of such forests rest in the hands of the individual owners or clans. While there is no official record as to the area covered by such forests in Lawbyrwa, they are of various sizes and densities depending on the owner's initiative and capabilities to maintain them. Some of them are well preserved and maintained with thick vegetational growth; evergreen trees and bamboo forests while majority of them are thin and poor in quality due to over-exploitation by the owners. It is a normal practice of these forest owners to cut down trees for timber, woodlots or charcoal making which is a major source of income of the villagers. During my field visits, some of the owner respondents expressed their genuine concern at the dwindling trend of their forests and their willingness to conserve forests for future harvest. Being by and large poor, however, they cannot afford to postpone operation. In recent times, a few of them have started replantation of trees, but it appears that the expertise in afforestation and Government initiative has not yet percolated down to this village inspite of the existence of the Umsning Development Block nearby.

Economic Profile of Lawbyrwa Village

Economy is often used as an important yardstick for measuring the degree of development of a particular society in different periods of history. The economy of Lawbyrwa village presents an interesting feature of a village that is still entirely forest based. Except for a few people who are engaged in trade and business and service in the MSEB office located within the village, the vast majority of the villagers eke out their livelihood from cultivation, charcoal making, cutting and selling firewood, collecting and selling of wild vegetables, broomshrubs, bamboo shoots, mushrooms etc. and from daily wages acquired through daily labour.

While dividing the sample households into three different income groups we find the following facts:

Table 6.4: Income Groups of Sample Households

Income Group	*Monthly Income (Rs.)*	*Annual Income (Rs.)*	*No. of house-holds*	*Percentage*
High	Above 8,000	96,000	6	10.00
Middle	4,000-8,000	48,000-96,000	14	23.34
Low	Below 4,000	Below 48,000	40	66.66
Total			60	100.00

Source: Fieldwork Data

The above table 6.4 reveals that the monthly family income ranges from Rs. 4,000 at the lowest to Rs. 8,000 at the highest. Amongst the High Income Group families comprising of only 6 families, only 1 (one) family has a high monthly salary of about Rs. 15,000 per month being employed in a government job and hence may be taken as exceptional. The remaining chunk of 40 households is engaged as marginal farmers, daily wage labourers and other subsidiary occupations. Speaking in terms of percentage we find that only 10 per cent of the sample households constitute the High Income Group, while a majority of 66.66 per cent constitute the Low Income Group.

An attempt was also made to find out the occupational background of the people of Lawbyrwa village. Out of a total of 208 households in the village, a sample of 60 households which forms approximately one-third of the total households were chosen which according to the investigator makes a fairly representative group of the village. These 60 households were comprised of a total of 180 working members, who also constitute the total number of respondents in the study.

In Table 6.5 furnished, an attempt has been made to examine the occupational distribution of the respondents in Lawbyrwa village:

Table 6.5: Occupational Distribution of Lawbyrwa Village

Sl. No.	*Occupation*	*Total No. of Respondents*	*Percentage*
1:	Agriculture	41	22.78
2.	Cutting Firewood	37	20.56
3.	Making Charcoal	40	22.22
4.	Collecting NTFP	31	17:23
5.	Daily Wage Labour	22	12.22
6.	Carpentry, Masonry	6	3.33
7.	Others	3	1.66
Total		**180**	**100.00**

Source: Fieldwork Data.

The occupational distribution of Lawbyrwa village reveals some interesting facts. Agriculture being the main occupation of the people in this village, the study reveals that 41 respondents out of a total of 180 are dependent on agriculture and related activities which accounts to 22.78 per cent of the total. This is followed by cutting timber for firewood, which amounts to 20.56 per cent. Charcoal making is another economic activity related to forest that amounts to 22.22 per cent followed by collection of Non-Timber Forest Products (NTFP) at 17.23 per cent. A small proportion of the village folks are engaged as daily wage labour at 12.22 per cent and carpentry and masonry within the village is at 3.33 per cent. A very small percentage of 1.65 per cent is comprised of people engaged in the MSEB office located within the village and as teachers in the local MSEB Higher Secondary School.

Agriculture

The primary occupation of the people of Lawbyrwa village is agriculture by way of shifting cultivation or slash and burn method of cultivation. By and large, adoption of new agricultural technology and practices appear to be negligible. The villagers continue to follow their traditional cultivation practices with the help of simple farm

Road Leading to Lawbyrwa Village

A View of Lawbyrwa Village

Shifting Cultivation on the Hill Slopes

Logs of Firewood for Making Charcoal

A Shed for Storing few Items of Forest Products

Vegetational Growth in the Village Forest

A Partial view of the Village Forest "Khlaw Shnong" at Lawbyrwa

A Partial view of a Private Forest Beloging to one of the Residents

The M.Seb Power Station Located at Lawbyrwa

The Author with One of the Oldest Respondents and her Grand Children

implements. They are engaged in cultivating rice, ginger, chillies, broomsticks, cucumber, etc. Temperate fruits like jackfruit, pineapple, mango, banana, and guava are also grown. The villagers, mostly men, leave their homes for their fields early in the morning and carry out the usual method of clearing the area and burning the bushes and trees, followed by planting of seeds on slopes without any knowledge of soil conservation.

The villagers generally follow the following jhum procedure:

1. Jungles are cut and cleared in the month of January.
2. After leaving them to dry, they are burned in the month of March.
3. Immediately the hills are prepared for sowing the seeds. Using simple farm equipments and human labour holes are dug in order to sow the seeds.
4. The crops are sown in April and there is no restriction to the kinds of crops sown because the farmers usually go for multiple cropping according to the season, the most common ones being ginger, chillies, cucumber, tomato, french beans, capsicum, pumpkin, hill paddy, etc.

The hill slopes used for *jhum* cultivation are then abandoned for a period of 3-4 years after which the same *jhum* site is used for carrying out the same process.

However, in order to get an answer to the question as to whether they are aware of the extent of devastation caused to forest by *jhuming*, all the respondents were asked as to why they continued to follow the traditional practice of cultivation. About 80 per cent of them replied that they accepted this method because it provided them with all their major food requirements with the benefits of multiple cropping. It also supplemented the economic needs of the family where every member of the family including children were involved in farming activities like weeding, digging holes, dibbling, clearing of shrubs and jungles, etc. An important feature noted during the fieldwork was that each household dependent on *jhum* cultivation was also aware of the importance of conserving the ecological balance, so they made sure that the *jhum* site could recuperate for re-*jhuming* after a few years by replanting quick growing trees in the same site.

Majority of the households in the village are either marginal or small cultivators, so the pressure on land is heavy and it was found that most of the respondents' households are not in a position to feel contended exclusively by depending on land. The average size of land holding by each respondent household is hardly 4-5 acres. Only a few households own lands larger than this. Further, other factors such as lack of chemical fertilizers and lack of new methods of agricultural practices have driven the poor farmers to resort to subsidiary occupations.

The entire cultivated land of the respondents lie within the village boundary. The cultivated land is generally divided into two: (1) Hilly land (*Ri Lum*); (2) Plain land (*Pynthor*). By and large both types of land are cultivable but the hilly lands being mostly covered with trees are generally left untouched except in cases where *jhum* activities are carried out, occasionally the jungles are cleared and the land is prepared for *jhum* cultivation. On the other hand, the plan areas (*Pynthor*) are extensively cultivated by dividing it into small plots of 2-3 acres and seasonal crops are grown through settled cultivation.

Felling Timber for Firewood

Lawbyrwa is predominantly a forested village with a forest area of 700 acres. The hill slopes alongside the village are well-covered with dense forest of bamboos, timber and other woody vegetation. Besides cultivation, the villagers earn their livelihood by felling trees for firewood. There is a good demand for firewood both in the local village market as well as outside. After the timber is felled and cut into logs of firewood, the villagers stake them in heaps locally called *Thak* measuring about 6 feet in length and 4 feet in breadth, in the dimension of each *thak* and tie them up in heaps ready to be sold. One *thak* of firewood is sold at Rs. 250 to Rs. 300 depending on the quality of wood. It is a common sight to see women and children carrying small landless of twigs and branches on their backs at the end of a long day at the woods. The fieldwork revealed that all the members of the family including the minors engaged themselves in collecting firewood, branches, and twigs from the jungles everyday to use as household energy. Firewood accounts for 100 per cent of the non-commercial energy consumed in the village.

Making Charcoal

Another predominant economic activity of the people of Lawbyrwa village is making charcoal by burning wood.

Charcoal making is a tedious process, which involves skill at every step. For the people who carry out this activity, the process comes naturally as they have been acquainted with it for a number of years. The following are the steps involved in charcoal making:

1. Firstly, logs of wood are felled.
2. The logs are then arranged according to their size and placed tightly one against another in deep pits, which are dug at a depth of about 2 feet below. The ground and the width vary according to the width of the logs.
3. The fire is then lighted from beneath the logs of wood and left to burn for a long time until the logs are fully burned and the mud from the walls of the pit start to fall on the burning logs and the fire is automatically put off.
4. After a week or 10 days the charcoal is taken out from the pit.

There is a high demand for charcoal in the markets. Truckloads of charcoal is produced in the villages in Khasi Hills and transported to Shillong and even to places outside Meghalaya. This is an activity mostly carried out by the landless forest families and farmers, who work on other's forest land during the lean seasons. There are also families in the village that let out their forest lands on hire to the daily labourers for charcoal operation. Some of these families on interview revealed that the used-up portion of their forest land was also taken care of by tree plantation and forest conservation practices.

So despite the fact that charcoal making is a rampant economic activity in Lawbyrwa village that could lead to a rapid degradation of forest cover in the years to come, it is heartening to note that there is some degree of awareness amongst a few families for conserving the forest by regeneration practices.

Fuelwood and charcoal are not merely used for cooking but also for warmth and lighting. All the families that were interviewed within the village did not have any other source of household energy for cooking other than fuelwood and charcoal. They are also dependent on charcoal to protect them from the cold winter.

The following Table 6.6 shows the pattern of household energy consumption in the village.

Table 6.6: Household Energy Consumption

Sl. No.	*Types of Household Energy Used*	*No. of Households*	*Percentage*
1.	Firewood and Charcoal	60	100.00
2.	Electricity	Nil	Nil
3.	Kerosene	Nil	Nil
4.	Other Non-Conventional Sources	Nil	Nil
Total		**60**	**100.00**

Source: Fieldwork Data.

Table 6.6 indicates a high dependency on firewood and charcoal for cooking and lighting. As far as the other means of household energy is concerned, it is surprising to note that none of the respondents' families make use of electricity as a household energy inspite of the fact that the MSEB office is located within the village and almost all the households in the village are connected with electricity.

Collecting Non-Timber Forest Products (NTFP)

The collection of items of daily use from the forest is another economic activity of Lawbyrwa village. The study revealed that nearly 60 per cent of elderly persons, 40 per cent of the children go to the forest daily for collection of tubers, leafy vegetables, bamboo shoots, mushroom and a host of other forest products. Not only the able-bodied worker but also the old and children bring something however modest it may be to the household, whereby they have the satisfaction of having contributed their mite. This ensures an inbuilt system of social security.

The young, old and women-folk for different purposes, mostly gather food items as well as other items of daily use. Table 6.7 shows the pattern of collection of forest foods and other forest products by the people of Lawbyrwa village.

Table 6.7: Purpose and Percentage of Persons Engaged in Forest Produce Collection

Sl. No.	Category	Food	For Construction Material	For Fuelwood	For Medicinal Purpose	For Sale in Market	Total Percentage
1.	Adult	55	31	36	5		100
2.	Children	22	16	18	Nil		

Source: Fieldwork Data.

Table 6.7 indicates that the villagers are to a great extent dependent on Non-Timber Forest Products for maintaining their household at a subsistence level. In case of certain items, a major part of their collection is for self-consumption. The edible products collected from the forest supplies them with a daily diet at the same time being conditioned by availability, marketability and easy access to forests. The monthly income derived from selling the collected forest products is a meagre amount, which is not sufficient to support the family.

The common food items sold are wild vegetables and fruits, roots, tubers, mushroom, etc. Construction material would include straw, grass and thatch, and other products such as fodder for cattle and broomsticks also form an important part of the collected forest products. Keeping in mind the important role of NTFP in the food and income budgets of the poor families of Lawbyrwa village, many of them are afraid of losing their right of collection without restrictions. As of now, the villagers are allowed to move freely in the jungles within the village without any restriction on their collection and marketing of the products.

Daily Wage Labour

Daily wage labour in the village is usually taken up side-by-side with other economic activities. The labourers working on others land are either engaged in farming activities like tilling the land, clearing the jungles, cutting firewood or cultivating the fields. The rates of daily wage are quite high, it being Rs. 80 per day for male workers and Rs. 60 per day for female workers. However, the demand for daily labour in the village itself is very low and the labourers hardly manage to get 10 days of work in a month.

Carpentry and Masonry

Carpentry and masonry works being an essential part of service in the society. Table 6.8 shows that only 6 respondents out of 110 were found to take up this activity. They build houses, make furniture out of timber. The daily wages vary from Rs. 180 to Rs. 130 per head. The high rate of wages is understandably due to the skill involved in the work and also scarcity of persons engaged in such works.

The economic profile of Lawbyrwa village reveals that although the villagers are mostly engaged in agricultural activity, a large chunk of the population also depends on forest for their living. They have resorted to subsidising occupations like collecting firewood, making charcoal, etc. for meeting their minimum requirements. It is seen that either the head of the household or any other adult member of the household, or sometimes both, take up subsidising occupations, unskilled manual labour, either on farm or in the forest is a common alternative during the lean season. Working, as labourers in the construction of roads and collecting non-timber forest products and bamboo products are other subsidiary activities. It is also revealed that majority of the villagers earn their livelihood from collection and sale of firewood and other NTFP. These are collected from the forest in the neighbourhood of the village for which there is a good market in the city of Shillong.

The nature of economic life of the people of Lawbyrwa village is thus marked by a relatively high degree of dependence on forest. Table 6.8 shows the high dependency on forest.

Table 6.8: Dependency on Forest

Sl. No.	*Occupation*	*No. of Persons Engaged*		*Percentage to Total*
1.	Agriculture	41		22.78
2.	Forest Activities:			
	(a) Cutting Firewood	37	108	60.00
	(b) Making Charcoal	40		
	(c) Collecting NTFP	31		
3.	Other activities	31		17.20
Total		**180**		**100.00**

Source: Fieldwork Data.

Table 6.8 on dependency on forest activities in Lawbyrwa village shows that respondents engaged in forest activities numbers to 108, which is the highest. This high dependency on forest activities forms an important feature of the study.

7

Profile of Madan Ïing Syiem Village

Madan Ïing Syiem village is located in the East Khasi Hills District of Meghalaya under Mylliem Development Block and falls within Mylliem syiemship. The village stands on National Highway No. 40 and it is situated at a distance of 16 kms. south of Shillong, the state capital of Meghalaya. This village has 185 households and a population of 1029 persons (2001 Census Report). Madan Ïing Syiem literally means 'home of the king' and it is one of the most ancient villages of Meghalaya. It was once the seat of administration of the Mylliem syiemship and presently, its durbar has been shifted to Shillong.

Madan Ïing Syiem village is one of the sample villages chosen for the present study on grounds that it satisfies the following three criterias as listed in the methodology, keeping in mind the objectives of my study:

1. It is a non-forested village with a marked departure from a forest-based economy tc a diversified one.
2. There are evidences of change in the socio-economic life of the villagers, which affords us to make a contrast study.

The total geographical area of Madan Ïing Syiem village is 2 sq. kms. with a population of 1029 persons and a total of 185 number of households as per the 2001 census data.

Table 7.1: Population Distribution of Madan Ïing Syiem Village

Sl. No.	Category	Populations
1.	Male	486
2.	Female	543
	Total	**1029**

Source: Mylliem Development Block (2001 Census).

Land and Geography

The village, situated towards the south of Shillong city is characterised by smooth hills and valleys running both towards the north and south with unknown parallel ranges. The altitude of the village is higher than that of Shillong city since it is situated uphill closer to the Shillong peak. The elevation difference between the hill top and valley floor is approximately 100-200 m. The entire village is hilly with smooth slopes, which are mostly under grass or shrub cover and small patches of forest land. A distinctive feature of the terrain is its almost barren hills with grassy plains and massive proportions of land slope. Narrow strips of valleys and terraced paddy fields are also found alongside streams.

The River System

Madan Ïing Syiem village has a number of rivers flowing from their source in the mountains but they are not perennial and remain dry during most part of the year. These rivulets are indicative of mountain torrents, thereby carrying in their force a large volume of deposit to enrich the soil in the valleys. Some of them form into cascades and waterfalls, which are a familiar sight on the roadside leading to the village.

There are three major rivers flowing across the village. They are Um Jlieng river, Um Jaliang river and Um Tang Syiem river. These rivers flow across the village providing a natural boundary, which clearly demarcates the village from the neighbouring villages.

Rainfall

The village receives moderate to high rainfall, the monsoon season normally starting from May to late August. Since a major part of the village is sloppy with undulating hills, thus, inspite of the heavy rainfall during monsoon, water drains out from the paddy fields. However, by and large the farmers do not have to depend on irrigation because the monsoon rains are sufficient.

Forest and Vegetation

The Khasi pine (*Pinus kesiya*) is the most extensive forest type found in the village. There are also patches of pure oak (*Dieng Kseh Bilat*) and associated species in the upper ranges of the hilltops. Due to the temperate cold climate in the higher altitude of the village, the vegetation cover is very sparse here. Bamboo thickets are found only in the lower ranges, which are mostly of secondary origin species.

The village once had thick forest cover but the increasing population pressure and resultant over exploitation of forests have taken a heavy toll of the forests. It has been almost 20-25 years since the forest cover was sufficiently available to meet the forest needs of the villagers. Today, Mylliem village is experiencing an extreme shortage of fuelwood, which is locally not available at all. Demand for fuelwood and wood for other purposes is met from outside the village.

There is a village forest covering an area of about 7 hectares, located on the outskirt of Madan Ïing Syiem village, which is commonly owned and managed by four surrounding villages including Madan Ïing Syiem. The four villages are combined to look into the management of the village forest. This forest caters to the common needs of the four villages for various community purposes.

Land Ownership and Land-use Pattern

Size of land owned is an important parameter of the social status of a family. Madan Ïing Syiem village stretches across a total land area of 210 hectares out of which 162 hectares is under cultivation. The percentage of cultivable land to total land is moderately high. The most striking feature of land ownership pattern of the village is that there are no Ri Raid lands or community land as found in other Khasi villages, but only Ri Kynti or private land, reason being that land as a commodity was either bought by private individuals or owned by clans and individual families. As such there has been no instance of land reverting back to the community due to its non-usage for three consecutive years, which is the accepted system of land-tenure among the Khasi. In the village, lands have been properly managed and protected by the private owners; most of whom rent out the lands for cultivation to the landless farmers for a stipulated period. From self-cultivation point of view, majority of the households in this village are either marginal or small cultivators and so they are not in a position to be economically self-sufficient by depending exclusively on agriculture alone. The average size of land holding per household is approximately 6 to 8 acre per household, which is quite high, but the entire land is not used for cultivation. Land not utilised by the owner is either given on rent for cultivation or left fallow for regeneration or fertility of the soil.

Table 7.2: Land Ownership Pattern

Sl. No.	*Amount of Land (Acres)*	*No. of Households*	*Percentage*
1.	Above 10 acres	15	25
2.	5-10 acres	18	30
3.	Up to 5 acres	19	32
4.	Landless families	8	13
	Total	60	**100**

Source: Fieldwork Data

Table 7.2 shows that the land ownership pattern in the village is almost evenly distributed amongst the residents, except for a small percentage of 13 per cent who are landless. Up to 25 per cent of the total households in the village own lands above 10 acres and 30 per cent hold land area of 5-10 acres. But it is remarkable that almost every household in the village owns a plot of land. This presents the village as a rural-based economy and it makes agriculture the primary occupation of the villagers here.

Land-use Patterns

Land for cultivation is of two types—Hilly land or '*Ri Lum*' and Plains or '*Pynthor*'. Cultivation of paddy is normally practised along the plains or '*pynthor*' while the hilly lands are used for cash crops cultivation. Land use in the village is associated with land ownership pattern. As most of the lands are owned privately, usage of land depends upon the capacity of the household members to use the lands according to their need. Most of the households who own lands cultivate only a portion of the total while the rest is not left fallow, because rotation of crops is also carried out, according to the season. A wide variety of seasonal crops are cultivated and so the lands are used accordingly from time to time, thus allowing it to recuperate its fertility.

It has also been found that the hilly lands or '*ri-lum*' are scantily covered with patches of pine trees (*Pinus kesiya*) and bamboo thickets while the plain valleys or '*pynthor*' are used for settled cultivation of paddy and food crops. While there is total absence of *jhum* cultivation practice in the village, the farmers make use of terrace cultivation in the slopes and settled cultivation in the plains. There are only few settlements on the hill slopes or near the paddy fields because majority of the farmers prefer to live in the village, which is in close proximity to their fields. The area of forest cover in the village is 10 hectares as against a total land area of 210 hectares which is very low and is one of the reasons why local felling of trees for firewood is strictly prohibited, nor do the villagers depend on forest related activities. The following Table 7.3 shows the pattern of land use in the village.

Table 7.3: Land Use Pattern in Madan Ïing Syiem

Sl. No.	*Pattern of Land Use*	*Total Area in Acres*	*Percentage to Total Area*
1.	Area under Cultivation	162	77.14
2.	Area under Settled Cultivation	32	15.24
3.	Area under Horticulture	6	2.86
4.	Area under *Jhum* Cultivation	Nil	–
5.	Area under Forest	10	4.76
	Total	**210**	**100.00**

Source: Village Gram Sevak (Block Office).

Infrastructure

The basic infrastructural facilities such as hospitals, markets, post office, college and so on. in the village are still far from being satisfactory but its closer distance to the city makes it easily accessible to facilities like markets, hospitals, schools, and colleges etc. which are making a fast changing influence in the life of the villagers.

Health

So far as health care is concerned, the village has no hospital or dispensary. The nearest Public Health Centre (PHC) is the Pomlum PHC located 8 kms. away from Madan Ïing Syiem. There is only one Health Care Clinic run by the Social Welfare Department, Government of Meghalaya, under the Mahila Mandal scheme. The clinic functions as a centre to supply medicines at a reasonable rate, it also runs a nursery school and a student nurse is employed at the clinic. There is also a private Doctor's clinic in the village where a doctor is available once a week every Saturday. This satisfies the basic medical needs of the villagers in the absence of which they would have to travel to the city for treatment.

Education

It is significant that the literacy rate of Madan Ïing Syiem village is fairly high compared to other villages in Khasi Hills. The present literacy rate of the village is 63.33 per cent. There are quite a number of well-educated residents within the village who have obtained their education from schools and colleges in Shillong.

There are four lower primary schools in the village, out of which, one is soon to be upgraded into a High School:

1. Hemont Zenith Primary School.
2. St. Mary's Girls School.
3. Per Sara School.
4. Lower Primary Government School.

Table 7.4: Educational background of Madan Ïing Syiem

Sl. No.	*Education Level*	*No. of Persons*	*Percentage*	*Total Literacy*
1.	Above Higher Secondary	14	7.78	
2.	Above Secondary	20	11.11	
3.	Primary Level	28	15.56	63.33
4.	Below Primary	52	28.89	
5.	Illiterate	66	36.67	
	Total	**180**	**100.00**	

Source: Fieldwork Data.

Government Offices

There are no Government institutions within the village itself. However, there are a number of offices in the outskirts of the village starting from 4½ mile to 7th mile on the Upper Shillong road which makes the village closer to them. They are:

1. Mylliem Development Block Office (5th Mile)
2. Office of the Assistant Conservator of Forest (4½ Mile)
3. Agriculture Office (6th Mile)
4. ICDS Office (5th Mile)
5. Convention Energy Office (5th Mile)
6. A.H. and Veterinary Office (5th Mile).

Economic Profile of Madan Ïing Syiem Village

The economy of the village is varied in occupational features. Though the primary occupation is agriculture, the villagers depend on a wide range of economic activities such as business and trade, cottage industries, daily labourers and even government service in petty jobs.

The following are the main occupation followed by the people of Madan Ïing Syiem village.

Agriculture

Agriculture is the primary occupation of the people of Madan Ïing Syiem village. The method of agriculture practice is still traditional. Use of improved agricultural implements, High Yielding Varieties (HYVs) of seeds and chemical fertiliser are not adopted. Unlike other tribal villages, the people never practise *jhum* cultivation. The lands are not left fallow for a long period and seasonal crops are grown according to season. The climate and soil conditions of the village are conducive to the cultivation of root crops like potato, carrot, radish and other vegetables.

Depending on the topography, three categories of land are available for cultivation—these are:

(1) Wet paddy land or "*pynthor*".

(2) Hilly land or "*Ri Lum*".
(3) Homestead land, or "*Ka Kper*".

Wet rice cultivation is practised on low lands called "*pynthor*". Such lands are situated on the foothills and are divided into compartments with the help of earthen banks that are locally called '*stir*'. This is done in order to retain rainwater.

The hilly lands or '*Ri lum*' are generally used for cultivation of potato and hill paddy. Potato may be considered as the cash crop of the Khasi insofar as it has become an extensive trading commodity for the people of this village.

Homestead lands are used by every household to grow vegetables and fruit trees like orange, plum, peach, etc. which they sell in the local markets. It has also been found that homestead lands yield better and produce more because personal care and attention is available.

The adoption of improved agricultural technology is negligible because the farmers still make use of traditional farm implements made of wood, bamboo and iron. The Khasi hoe called "*U Mohkhiew*", an axe for felling trees and shrubs "*U sdie*", a sickle "*Ka rashi*" and a harrow "*Ka ïuh moi*" are used. For manuring the fields, the farmers use *"sboh sem masi"* (lumps of decomposed cowdung) and "*sboh sem sniang*" (pig sty), while the use of chemical fertilizers is not prevalent. The winter crops that govern the yearly cycle of all activities include potatoes, radish, cauliflower, carrots, green leafy vegetables and beans. Paddy is sown in early April and by winter they collect the sheaves and start thrashing out on the spot by beating them against stone (*shoh kba*) both by men and women.

The land use pattern of the village also shows a high percentage of cultivable land, 77 per cent or 162 hectares as against a total land area of 210 hectares, which makes agriculture the primary economic activity of the village.

Businesses and Trading

A sizeable number of the villagers are engaged in various petty business activities like running tea shops, restaurants and general grocery stores, etc. This is mainly because of the location of the village on the national highway that connects Cherrapunjee, which is an important place of tourist interest and a passage to Bangladesh. Tourists and travellers passing by this route often stop for a while and take tea or food in these tea stalls.

This has become a lucrative business and it is a common sight to see tired travellers especially tourists on their way to Cherrapunjee halting by these tea shops and enjoying a cup of hot tea with locally prepared Khasi specialities like '*pu-tharo*' and "*pu-khleiñ* (rice pancakes). Besides tea shops, the other business activities in the village include tyre repair shops, carpentry, general stores and a few local wine dealers.

Table 7.5 shows the percentage distribution of business activities in Madan Ïing Syiem village.

Table 7.5: Distribution of Business Activities

Sl. No.	*Business Activities*	*Number*	*Percentage*
1.	Tea Stall	30	51.72
2.	General Store	20	34.48
3.	Cement Dealer	4	6.89
4.	Charcoal Seller	4	6.89
	Total	**58**	**100.00**

Source: Fieldwork Data.

Iron Smelting or Shlem Saiñ Nar Mawpyrsut

Iron smelting is one of the chief industries in the Khasi Hills and Madan Ïing Syiem village has earned a name for itself as one of the oldest centres of this industry. W.W. Hunter in his *Statistical Account of Assam* 1879 wrote:

> "The smelting of iron was once the chief industry in the Khasi Hills, and a considerable quantity of the metal used to be exported to Sylhet, both in the crude and manufactured state. Recently, however, this industry has almost died out, in the face of the competition of the superior article imported from England and sold in the plains at a cheaper rate."

Many early writers have commented upon this industry, which was indigenous to the Khasi since time immemorial such as Colonel

Lister, Yale, Cracroft and Thomas Oldham. Colonel Lister reported that in 1853, the estimated quantity of 20,000 mounds of iron in the shape of hoes was exported from the hills to the Assam valley (Choudhury, 1978: 66).

Besides Nongkrem and Laitlyngkot which are known as centres of iron industry in the Khasi Hills, Madan Ïing Syiem village is also a centre of iron industry still being pursued on a large scale for producing the typical Khasi hoe called *u Moh-khiew* and various types of Khasi dao or *wait.*

Method of Khasi Blacksmithy in Madan Ïing Syiem

It is interesting to note that the local blacksmiths of this village still use the ordinary hand-driven bellows. The ancient cottage industry is carried out in primitive charcoal fires, which are blown by huge double action bellows. On the side of the bellow is a nozzle through which is inserted a tube connecting the hearth. Over the hearth is a chimney of pipe clay to direct the heated air from the smelter to the opening in the roof. In Madan Ïing Syiem there are 2 iron cottage industries which produce various iron implements for daily use such as knives, swords, spades and a number of Khasi 'daos' such as *wait bnoh* or the hooked dao, *wait lyngkut* or curved dao, *wait kynda* or warrior's knife, *wait sum* or butcher's knife, *tari dao* or kitchen knife, etc. and the Khasi hoe or *mohkhiew*. These household and agricultural implements are bought by traders in bulk and sold at Barabazar, Shillong and various interior markets.

Carpentry

Carpentry as an economic activity also finds place in the economic life of the villagers, but there are only 2 furniture making centres in the village. The carpenters have to purchase wood from outside the village, which are heavily priced by the dealers. Most of the timber comes from West Khasi Hills in truckloads and are sold in the local markets or saw mill located at Upper Shillong (Lai Mer). Each carpentry shop owner employs about 3 to 4 skilled labourers who are engaged in different activities like sawing, polishing, etc. The labourers are paid Rs. 100 per day. All types of furniture for daily use are made such as tables, beds, chairs, doors, windows, etc. Depending upon the type of wood, the prices are fixed at varied rates, some of which are available on placement of order. There is no local wood available for sale, and it has been a regular practice in the village for the past 20-25 years that firewood has to be purchased from outside.

Distributing the total adult working population of the village we find the following broad occupational pattern of Madan Ïing Syiem village.

Table 7.6: Broad Occupational Pattern of Madan Ïing Syiem

Sl. No.	Occupation	No. of Adults engaged	Percentage to Total
1.	Cultivation	72	40.00
2.	Traders	58	32.22
3.	Forest Activities (carpentry)	5	2.78
4.	Cottage Industry	15	8.33
5.	Service	10	5.56
6.	Labour	20	11.11
	Total	**100**	**100.00**

Source: Fieldwork Data.

Table 7.6 holds out, as it is, the predominance of agriculture, which engages 72 out of 180 adult working members of the households accounting for 40 per cent of the workers. The next occupation significantly distinctive to this village is trade and business. This occupies as many as 58 adults amounting to 32.22 per cent. In sharp contrast to the other sample village Lawbyrwa, forest activity in this village is conspicuously nil. Employment of 10 persons in Government services and school teaching also indicates some degree of educational advancement.

Self-Help Groups (SHGs)

These Self-Help Groups are sponsored by the Soil and Water Conservation Department of the Government of Meghalaya. The formation of a number of Self-Help Groups (SHGs) has been an important means of employment opportunity for the villagers.

There are in total 5 SHGs in Madan Ïing Syiem village organized by the Soil and Water Conservation Department, East Khasi Hills

District, under its Watershed Development Programme (WDP) scheme. It was observed that all these groups have built up a creditable system in which every member gets trained to take collective responsibility without depending on one individual. Although the levels of knowledge, skills, understanding differ from one group to another either within or outside the village watershed areas, concentrated efforts by certain individuals and nurturing of those groups was found to be far more important than formation of such groups.

Table 7.7 shows the number of SHG's in Madan Ïing Syiem village, their membership and their activities and achievements.

Table 7.7: Profile of Self-Help Groups in Madan Ïing Syiem

Sl. No.	*Name of the SHG*	*Date & Year of Formation*	*Total No. of Members*	*Activities and Achievements*
1.	Bankyrsoi Self-Help Group	24.07.03	11	(1) Social work which include cleaning of the village every year on the 2nd Oct. which coincides with Mahatma Gandhi's birthday. (2) Started Mushroom cultivation with financial assistance of Rs. 10,000 from Soil Conservator.
2.	Nangkyntiew Shaphrang Self-Help Group	27.08.02	13 (all women) Membership Fee	(1) In the first coaching year, the group started cultivation of vegetables and daily wage labour and the money earned was kept in the Bank. The group started selling iron to the backsmiths in the village.
3.	Lawei Baphyrnai Self-Help Group	05.05.03	12 (women) Membership Fee—20 per month	(1) To give loans to each and every member in the group from their own revolving fund.

(*Contd.*)

Table 7.7 (*Contd.*)

Sl. No.	*Name of the SHG*	*Date & Year of Formation*	*Total No. of Members*	*Activities and Achievements*
4.	Shilynter Self-Help Group	03.06.04	11 (50 each)	(1) Giving loans to the members
5.	Nangkiew Shaphrang	01.03.02	12 (20 each)	(1) In the first year the group started cultivation of vegetables and the sale proceeds was kept in the Bank. (2) Received a grant of Rs. 10,000 from Soil Conservation Division to make Vern compost.

Source: Report of Soil and Water Conservation Department, 15th June 2005, on Self-Help Groups in different Watershed Development Programmes under Divisional Soil and Water Conservation Division, Shillong.

It has been observed that the efforts made by the Soil and Water Conservation Department in Madan Ïing Syiem village are encouraging and helpful. Through decentralization of decision making process and empowerment of existing village institutions namely Watershed Association, Watershed Committee, Self-Help Groups, User Groups, etc. financially and socially there is a ray of hope that at one point of time they may become viable to take up development process on their own. Training camps are also organised by the State Institute of Rural Development (SIRD) and Community and Rural Development Block to enlighten the villagers on the management of the investments and also to provide opportunities to interact.

The Self-Help Groups, under the guidance and supervision of the Soil and Water Conservation Department, will go a long way to help the village folk in developing them confidence and skill to work collectively for their economic welfare.

It will also help them for better access to resources, credits and other required inputs in achieving their desired goals. The Watershed Development Programme is a scheme funded by the Government of India under the Ministry of Agriculture and is mainly directed towards the overall development of *jhum* areas of the watershed basis by way of reclaiming the land offered by shifting cultivation and thereby to bring about socio-economic upgradation of the *jhumia* families living in these areas. This scheme, if properly implemented, is sure to benefit the Khasi farmers who are traditionally dependent on *jhum* cultivation. The Department of Soil and Water Conservation, Meghalaya, which initiated the promotion of Self-Help Group schemes claims that the SHG's are slowly picking up with greater involvement in credit-cum subsidy programme that would ensure a time bound programme for bringing a specific member of families now under Below Poverty Line (BPL) out of their chronic poverty and deprivation.

Daily Labourers

Daily labourers constitute an important segment in the area of study. There are basically 4 categories of daily labourers in Madan Ïing Syiem village. They are:

(i) Stone crusher (*Shoh maw*)
(ii) Sand Tiller (*Tih Shyïap*)
(iii) Muster Roll in road construction (*Bylla surok*)
(iv) Landless labourers. (*Bylla sngi*)

While menfolk are usually employed in the first three categories, women also engage themselves in such activities though in lesser numbers.

In the foregoing Table 7.7 under the heading "Broad Occupational Pattern of Madan Ïing Syiem", the number of persons under the category of 'Labour' has been shown as 20 with 11.11 per cent of the total number of adult workers. They are mostly landless labourers who work with others on daily wages. While it sounds paradoxical to find landless persons in a country where land belongs to the people, needless to say, the process of land alienation that has been increasingly taking place in Khasi Hills since last few decades this class of landless persons is gradually increasing.

Use of Fuelwood as Household Energy

In any study of the usages of forest and forest products, one of the important considerations that come to the forefront is the consumption of firewood as household energy. Like any other tribe, the Khasis traditionally use firewood as the medium for cooking and heating. Charcoal is extensively used for various domestic requirements like warming themselves during winter season, cooking, and for drying up clothes in monsoon. Even the core of the roots of matured pine comes handy for lighting purposes.

It is a usual practice of Khasis to collect firewood from the forest during the dry season beginning from January to March and to stack them for cooking, heating and warming themselves during the wet seasons. Every household of average size (4 to 6 persons) must have a provision of one '*thup*' of firewood for the year. '*Thup*' or '*Thak*' is a local name given for a stake of firewood approximately weighing 10 quintals or about one-jeep-trailor load. Calculating on the basis of the above estimate it will be seen that the annual consumption of firewood by 60 numbers of households will come to 600 quintals.

With a view to find out whether this heavy requirement of fuelwood has been reduced by supplementing it with other sources of energy like electricity, kerosene and non-conventional energies, a study was made on our sample village—Madan Ïing Syiem.

The data collected in this regard are expressed in Table 7.8.

Table 7.8: Household Energy Consumption in Madan Ïing Syiem

Sl. No.	*Types of Energy Used*	*Number of Households*	*Percentage*
1.	Firewood	60	100.00
2.	Electricity	10	41.66
3.	Kerosene	15	
4.	Other sources	Nil	—

Source: Fieldwork Data.

Table 7.8 reveals that all the 60 households, the entire families or 100 per cent households still use firewood as their primary source of energy. However, they have also started using other sources of energy such as electricity, kerosene and charcoal to supplement the daily requirements of firewood to the extent of 41.66 per cent in Madan Ïing Syiem. This fact indicates two things: (1) scarcity of firewood in the village and (2) higher cost of firewood. This has a sharp contrast with the other sample village, i.e., Lawbyrwa.

Monthly Income of Households

The economic status of a family or household reflects on the actual income it earns, it was thus considered important to collect, assess and analyse the monthly income of each family of the sample village in order to explore the socio-economic structure under the changing scenario. One of the objectives of the present study being exploring the emerging socio-economic structure of the Khasis under the changing harmony between the Khasi and the forest, in this study an attempt has been made to bring out, as accurate as possible, the monthly income of the 60 households under study from all sources.

In Table 7.9, the households have been grouped under three different categories of High, Middle and Low income groups to make it convenient to express the income in terms of amount and percentages for comparative study between two sample villages.

Table 7.9: Household Income of Madan Ïing Syiem

Sl. No.	*Income Groups*	*Monthly Income*	*No. of Households*	*Percentage*
1.	High	Above Rs. 8000	12	20.00
2.	Middle	Between Rs. 8000 to 4000	33	55.00
3.	Low	Below Rs. 4000	15	25.00
Total			60	100.00

Source: Fieldwork Data.

Table 7.9 reveals that the majority of the households fall under the Middle income group with 33 households out of 60 under review. The second category of Low income group includes 15 households and the third category of High income group has only 12 households with 55, 25 and 20 per cent respectively.

8

Comparative Study of Socio-economic Profiles between the two Sample Villages

While the foregoing two chapters provided an analysis of the socio-economic dynamics of the two sample villages, i.e., Lawbyrwa and Madan Ïing Syiem on the basis of the data collected through fieldwork, this chapter puts them in close juxtaposition so as to bring out the relative differences within the socio-economic parameters.

Geography and the People

Lawbyrwa is a forested village with a population of 655 persons and a geographical area of 15 sq. km. while Madan Ïing Syiem has an area of 125 sq. km with a population of 1029 persons. The former lies to the north of Shillong, the state capital, at a distance of 22 km. and away from the National Highway while the latter is only 16 km. to the south of Shillong and is located just on the National Highway No. 40. The location of the two villages has contributed to their comparative socio-economic differences.

The people of both the villages are predominantly Khasi Christians with scanty admixture of non-tribal people. Educationally, they differ vastly from each other, Lawbyrwa with only 23.89 per cent of literacy and Madan Ïing Syiem with a more advanced literacy rate of 63.33 per cent. Table 8.1 exhibits the differences.

Table 8.1: Educational Background

Sl. No.	*Educational Level*	*Lawbyrwa*		*Madan Ïing Syiem*	
		No. of persons	*Percentage*	*No. of persons*	*Percentage*
1.	Higher Secondary	1	0.56	14	7.78
2.	High School	3	1.67	20	11.11
3.	Primary	12	6.67	28	15.56
4.	Below Primary	27	15.00	53	28.89
5.	Illiterate	137	76.11	66	36.67
6.	Total literates	43	23.89	114	63.33
	Total	**180**	**100.00**	**180**	**100.00**

The average literacy rate of Meghalaya state being 63.31 (Census 2001), Table 8.1 shows that Lawbyrwa has literacy rate much below the average of the state while Madan Ïing Syiem has slightly higher than that of the state average. We also find from Table 8.1 that there is only one person (0.56 per cent) having education above Higher Secondary level in Lawbyrwa village as against 14 persons (7.78 per cent) of the same educational level in Madan Ïing Syiem. The wider gulf of difference in educational levels inevitably casts a reflection upon the socio-economic and cultural situations of the two villages which reveals that Lawbyrwa still retains the rural scenario of a traditional Khasi village while Madan Ïing Syiem is moving ahead with traces of modernity. Literacy and education may be regarded as an important criterion to reflect the progress of an individual and the society as a whole. According to Census Report of the Government of India, the percentage of literates in the State of Meghalaya has considerably risen up and its rank at the all-India level is at 27th position. It is interesting to note that the male and female ratio in literacy is almost equal, the male percentage being 66.14 and the female 60.41 during 2001 Census.

Table 8.2 gives the growth of literacy in the State of Meghalaya since 1971 to 2001.

As regards educational facilities, the village Lawbyrwa has one Lower Primary, one Middle English and one High School and therefore, for higher education at the college and university level, the students have to come to Shillong. The other village, Madan Ïing Syiem, has three private and missionary primary schools and one proceeding high school besides its proximity and good transport facilities to come to Shillong for higher studies.

Table 8.2: Literacy Rate in Percentage

Particulars	*1971*	*1981*	*1991*	*2001*
Rural	23.40	27.45	41.05	57.00
Urban	65.22	64.12	81.74	87.19
Total	29.49	34.08	49.10	63.31
Male	34.12	37.89	53.12	66.14
Female	24.56	30.08	44.85	60.41

Source: Directorate of Economics and Statistics, Meghalaya, Meghalaya Socio-Economic Review, *2003.*

Land and Land Ownership

As in other parts of the country, where Land is the primary source of livelihood and its ownership is the well-accepted indicator of the farmer's socio-economic status, this norm is equally applicable in Khasi Hills but the problem arises in the difficulty to estimate the area of land possessed by each household. Unlike other parts of the country, Khasi Hills do not have a cadastral survey map of each village. In the absence of such cadastral survey and accurate measurements of land, it is difficult to give the exact quantity of land possessed by each family. It was also found through fieldwork, that most of the farmers do not have a fair knowledge about the standard of land measurement. Therefore, the figures quoted in this study are only indicative and not accurate. However, utmost care has been taken so that the land areas estimated are nearest to accuracy.[1]

To understand the land ownership pattern of the two sample villages households were divided into four categories. The first category of households having more than 10 acres as well-to-do groups and the last category of households having no land at all, as the landless farmers and the two categories of households possessing 1 to 10 acres as the middle income group families.

In Lawbyrwa village out of 60 households only 6 or 10 per cent of the households own lands above 10 acres, while in Madan Ïing Syiem village as many as 15 households or 25 per cent of the households own land above 10 acres. This shows comparatively better economic security and well-being of the families of Madan Ïing Syiem. This indicates that there is a sizeable number of landless families in both villages. Out of 60 households 12 are landless families in Lawbyrwa village while 8 families are landless in Madan Ïing Syiem. Thus, the incidence of landlessness appears to be very high in both villages. In a tribal society like that of the Khasis where land belongs to the people (*Raid Land*) landlessness is an anathema which is apt to cause concern to all social scientists, economists and the planners. The situation calls for a deeper research and study about the causes and effects of the ongoing processes of land alienation in Khasi Hills. The situation also throws ample light on the enormity of the deprivation of land as a natural resource and the resultant economic insecurity of the Khasi indigenous tribals. In the concluding chapter that follows we have made an attempt at dealing with this crucial subject at some length.

Table 8.3: Landownership Pattern

Sl. No.	*Quantity of Land (Acres)*	*Lawbyrwa*		*Madan Ïing Syiem*	
		No. of Households	*Percentage*	*No. of Households*	*Percentage*
1.	Above 10 acres	6	10.00	15	25.00
2.	5 to 10 acres	12	20.00	18	30.00
3.	1 to 5 acres	30	50.00	19	32.00
4.	Landless households	12	20.00	8	13.00
	Total	**60**	**100.00**	**60**	**100.00**

Land-use Pattern

The socio-economic dynamics of the two villages reveals a significant revelation about the contrast and diversity in their practice of *jhum* cultivation. It is seen that *jhum* cultivation, the traditional method of agricultural operation, is still carried out in village Lawbyrwa on a large scale while it is absolutely negative in Madan Ïing Syiem. The land used for *jhum* cultivation in Lawbyrwa is 19.23 per cent while it is nil in Madan Ïing Syiem.

Table 8.4 Land Use Pattern

Sl. No.	*Patterns of Land Use*	*Lawbyrwa*		*Madan Ïing Syiem*	
		Area in acres	*Percentage*	*Area in acres*	*Percentage*
1.	Cultivated land	300	23.07	167	77.14
2.	*Jhum* cultivation	250	19.23	Nil	Nil
3.	Settled cultivation	50	3.85	32	15.24
4.	Horticulture	0	—	6	2.86
5.	Forest	700	53.85	10	4.76
	Total	**1300**	**100.00**	**210**	**100.00**

The contrast in *jhum* cultivation between the two villages is explained by the use of land under forest. Lawbyrwa is a forested village with 700 acres or 53.85 per cent of the village area under forest while Madan Ïing Syiem has barely 10 acres of its land covered by forest. *Jhum* cultivation or *Thang Shyrti* being the traditional and primitive way of cultivation of the Khasis, the non-existence of this practice in Madan Ïing Syiem marks a revealing departure from their time-honoured culture. The empirical evidences available, indicates the predominance of agriculture in the land use pattern of both the villages with 23.07 per cent in Lawbyrwa and 77.14 per cent in Madan Ïing Syiem and a gradual shift from *jhum* cultivation to settled cultivation in both villages with 3.85 per cent and 15.27 per cent of land use respectively.

Broad Occupational Pattern

Occupationally agriculture continues to occupy a predominant place in both the villages although trade and business have attracted some sections of the society in Madan Ïing Syiem. About 23.98 per cent of the adults of Lawbyrwa village and 40 per cent of Madan Ïing Syiem are currently engaged in agriculture. However, the occupational shift is clearly visible in both the villages. In Lawbyrwa the occupation is based on forest activities as primary source of livelihood, while in Madan Ïing Syiem the shift is from agro-economy to macro-economy based on trade and business—the former economy being narrow and closed while the latter broad and open. In Lawbyrwa, as many as 60 per cent of the adult workers are engaged in forest activities. On the other hand Madan Ïing Syiem shows absolutely no sign of any individual practising forest activities.

Table 8.5: Broad Occupational Pattern

Sl. No.	*Occupation*	*Lawbyrwa*		*Madan Ïing Syiem*	
		No. of adults engaged	*Percentage*	*No. of adults engaged*	*Percentage*
1.	Agriculture	43	23.89	72	40.00
2.	Trade/Business	Nil	Nil	58	28.22
3.	Forest Activities	108	60.00	Nil	Nil
4.	Cottage Industries	6	3.33	15	10.33
5.	Government Service	3	1.67	10	7.56
6.	Labour	20	11.11	25	13.89
	Total	**180**	**100.00**	**180**	**100.00**

While agriculture is the primary occupation in both the sample villages, the agricultural practice followed is primitive and traditional. The cultivators depend on the monsoon for the supply of water to paddy fields and other wet cultivation. If the monsoon fails, the farmers have to face various problems. Use of fertilizers and improved variety of seeds are still not adopted by the people. The principal crops grown in Lawbyrwa are rice, maize, potato, beans, pumpkin, chillies, etc. while potato is the main crop grown in Madan Ïing Syiem. The methods of cultivation followed in Lawbyrwa is traditional turfing (*thang bun*) in which the soil is heaped and turfed and the sods are extracted and left to dry after which, they are burned. The ashes are levelled down and soil is heaped before the seed is sown. Potato thrives best in this practice.

The forest activities in Lawbyrwa which engages 60 per cent of the adult population consists of (1) felling and collecting timber for firewood; (2) making charcoal out of wood and selling them, and (3) collecting Non-Timber Forest Products (NTFP) like wild fruits and vegetables, roots, tubers, mushrooms, etc. largely from season to season. Daily wage labour as an occupation engages 11.11 per cent people of Lawbyrwa and 13.29 per cent of Madan Ïing Syiem and the nature of work, by and large, consists of farming activities like tilling of land, clearing jungle, cutting firewood, and carrying goods. The rates of daily wages are considerable high in both the villages being Rs. 80 per day for adult male and Rs. 60 per day for adult female.

Taking a look at the forest activities of Lawbyrwa village it can be understood by the following sub-divisions into 3 broad categories for which data was collected to find out the number of persons dependent in each category.

Table 8.6: Dependency on Forest Activities of Lawbyrwa Village

Sl. No.	*Forest Activity*	*No. of Dependents*	*Percentage to total Workers*	*Total Adult Workers*
1.	Cutting firewood	37	20.56	
2.	Making Charcoal	40	22.22	180
3.	Collecting NTFP	31	17.22	
			60.00	dependent on
	Total	108	+ 40.00	Agri. & other activities
			Total 100.00	

It is seen that 60 per cent of the total 180 adult workers are engaged in three different forest activities and the balance of 40 per cent workers follow agriculture and other activities in the village. Among these three categories of forest related activities, charcoal making engages the maximum number of persons (40), cutting firewood stands second at 37 and collecting Non-Timber Forest Products (NTFP) engaging 31 persons.

Household Energy Consumption

Traditionally, the Khasis depend heavily on firewood for their daily requirement of household energy for cooking, heating, warming and drying purposes.[2] Of late, however, due to scarcity of firewood many Khasi families have shifted to alternative sources of energy such as electricity, kerosene and other non-conventional sources.

In both the villages, the households were given four alternatives and were asked to indicate their preferences in respect of daily use of energy. The alternatives were firewood, electricity, kerosene and other non-conventional energies. Table 8.7 shows the choice of energy consumption of the two sample villages.

In both the villages the households still use firewood and charcoal for purposes of cooking, boiling, heating, warming, etc. In Lawbyrwa, the use of firewood/charcoal is exclusive and no other energy source is used by them. In Madan Ïing Syiem 25 households or 41.66 per cent use electricity and kerosene as supplementary to firewood, thereby reducing the pressure on firewood. Firewood is locally not available in this village. It is brought by wholesale traders from interior villages by trucks and sold at an exhorbitant rate of Rs. 200 for 80 pieces of splitted logs of 4″ × 24″ size approximately. Cooking of food is normally done by firewood as the Khasis are averse to use other energy in preparing their food, while heating and warming up are gradually shifting towards kerosene and electricity. They also use charcoal alternatively for all these purposes.

Table 8.7: Household Energy Consumption

Sl. No.	*Type of Energy Used*	*Lawbyrwa*		*Madan Ïing Syiem*	
		No. of Households	*Percentage*	*No. of Households*	*Percentage*
1.	Firewood/Charcoal	60	100.00	60	100.00
2.	Electricity	Nil	Nil	10 } 25	
3.	Kerosene	Nil	Nil	15 } 25	41.66
3.	Kerosene	Nil	Nil	Nil	
	Total	**60**	**100.00**	**60**	**100.00**

Monthly Income of the Households

Evaluating and understanding the income of a household is an important index of any socio-economic study, because it reflects the levels of economic well-being or the status of the family or the society in which one lives. At the same time, the work of assessing the monthly or annual income out of multifarious activities and sources of income in terms of money is the most difficult task before any field worker. This is more true in respect of villagers who hardly keep any account of their earning and lack in domestic budgetary planning. An utmost care was therefore, taken while evaluating and assessing their out-turns so that the findings are as nearly accurate as possible. For this purpose, the values of their agricultural yields and other out-turns were evaluated in terms of money on the basis of prevailing market rates and in case of wage earners their actual number of working days were multiplied by the local rates of daily wage.

Table 8.8 gives us an overall picture of the economic conditions of the villages. In table, the households have been grouped under three categories of high, middle and low income groups to show their monthly income ranges with the number of households and percentages.

Table 8.8: Monthly Income of Households

Sl. No.	*Income Groups*	*Monthly Income Ranges*	*Lawbyrwa*		*Madan Ïing Syiem*	
			No. of households	*Percentage*	*No. of households*	*Percentage*
1.	High	Above Rs. 8000	6	10.00	12	20.00
2.	Middle	Rs. 4000 to 8000	14	23.33	33	55.00
3.	Low	Below Rs. 4000	40	66.67	15	25.00
	Total		**60**	**100.00**	**60**	**100.00**

The above Table 8.8 indicates an overwhelmingly large number of households of Lawbyrwa village, i.e., 40 out of 60 households or 66.67 per cent of them are poor families whose monthly income from all sources are below Rs. 4000. The position of Madan Ïing Syiem is comparatively better off with only 15 households or 25 per cent of the families under the lowest income group. Among the middle income groups, whose income is between Rs. 4000 to Rs. 8000 per month, the position of Madan Ïing Syiem is noteworthy with 33 households out of 60, or in other words 55 per cent which is more than half of the total number of families that fall within this group as against a meagre 14 households in Lawbyrwa. At the highest level of income group we find only 6 households (10%) whose monthly income ranges above Rs. 8000 per month in Lawbyrwa as against reasonably higher number of households, i.e., 20 per cent (double) in Madan Ïing Syiem. All these data unmistakably point out to the fact that the present day open and diversified economy definitely outweigh the traditional agro-forest based economy. This is because the former has a widening and unlimited scope while the latter is sumscribed within a small and limited sphere. In the foregoing paragraphs we have seen that the occupational pattern of the village Lawbyrwa is centred round forest and agricultural activities while Madan Ïing Syiem has a shift from agronomy to macro-economy based on trade and business.

Notes

1. Each respondent has been shown an exemplary area of land as a unit measurement and asked to estimate as to how many times as big is his area of land.
2. They use charcoal also for warning themselves during winter and heating purposes.

9

Summary and Conclusion

The Khasi are a people who live in profound communion with nature. Their home, the Khasi Hills which is known as the 'Meghalaya Plateau' or the 'central plateau' is abound in rich evergreen forests. Its topography with varied attitudes, temperate and semi-tropical nature of climate, characterised by abundant rainfall lasting almost half of the year have helped quick and luxuriant growth of wide varieties of trees and plants of extraordinary sizes and heights, shrubs and green vegetation all over the district. Trees like Khasi pine (*Pinus iusularis*) grow in abundance in major parts of central region while other non-conifer trees (broad leaved) like teak, sal, segun, etc. grow in lower altitudes. Chir-pine (*Pinus voxburghi*) and Deodar also grow in some areas. Khasi Hills produce many varieties of commercial timber like Titachampa (*Mechelia champaca*), Bonsum (*Phoebe goalparensis*), Gamari (*Gamelina arboria*), Bola (*Morus laevigate*), Nahar (*Mesua ferren*) etc. Besides these, many other minor forests like bamboo, small timber, woodlot, thatch, broom grass occur extensively. Thus nature has, over the past many hundred years of maintenance, regeneration and balanced sustainability of eco-system, turned Khasi Hills into a veritable home for the Khasis to live in the midst of natural bounty.

While the main focus of this book has been on the traditional usages of forest and forest products amongst the Khasis, it also takes a look at the role of forest in Khasi livelihood and the emerging trend and transition that has taken place in the Khasi socio-economic scenario with regard to forest.

Three pertinent issues have emerged out of the field study that was conducted in the two sample villages:

1. The forest continues to hold an important place in the life and culture of the Khasis.
2. There has been an infringement on the people's traditional rights over forest.
3. There is a gradual but inevitable shift in the Khasi economy from forest based livelihood to a diversified economy.

Forest Continues to Hold an Important Place in the Life and Culture of the Khasis

The forest occupies a central place in the socio-cultural and economic life of the Khasis. Conservation of natural resources is embedded in the ethos of Khasi life and culture. Ever since the time when they were hunter-cum-gatherers, they have maintained a deep symbiotic relationship with their natural environment, which have played a dominant role determining their way of life. The indelible mark that the forest had left on the Khasi thought, behaviour and attitude, can clearly be seen today in their culture, customs and religion. In many of these legends, folklores, songs and dances, this rapport with nature and environment comes out forcefully. For a Khasi, the forest, which is a well loved home, a game sanctuary and storehouse of everything he needs, has entered the *sanctum-sanctorum* of the Khasi religious rites and rituals including many social ceremonies.

The indigenous system of folk medicine made out of plants and herbs, which is prevalent among the Khasi society accounts for the rich ecological heritage of the Khasis over the centuries. The Khasis have developed an indigenous ethno-medical knowledge, which has served the Khasi community well even to this day. A study conducted by the North Eastern Biodiversity Research Cell of NEHU, Shillong, revealed that the total volume of medicinal plants or their products used or consumed per year was 80 to 120 tonnes, involving an amount of Rs. 2.5 crore per annum within three districts of Khasi and Jaintia Hills.

The present work also brings into focus the unique system of traditional forest management among the Khasis. The study revealed three different types of traditional forests, viz. (i) *Law Kyntang* (Sacred Grove); (ii) *Law Adong* or *Law Shnong* (Protected or Village Forest) and (iii) *Law Sumar* (Private Forest) which are preserved, controlled and managed by the village authority, individual or clan, as the case may be. It exhibits a deep sense of eco-consciousness and the ecological wisdom of the Khasi forefathers about the value of forests for the general well being of the community as a whole. Scientists have appreciated that a forest cover influences climate and soil conditions and increases underground storage of water. This fact seems to have been known to the Khasi ancestors who practised the system of maintaining forest around their villages. Blocks of dark and deep forests are visible even today in the outskirts of every village nearest to the source of water for drinking and washing clothes. The existence of these centuries' old forests speaks of rich eco-heritage of the Khasis, and their close affinity with nature.

For a Khasi, 'God', 'Man' and 'Nature' form one single entity. This eco-theandric view also personifies natural objects like rivers, streams, hills and mountains as God. The *Law Kyntang* (Sacred Grove) is a forest dedicated to God, where the Khasi priests perform rituals, pay homage and offer sacrifices to appease the spirits. The sacred groves are looked upon as holy, venerable and scary and no one is allowed to enter into it and damage or cut any tree. Thus the forests signify a sense of eco-spirituality among the Khasis borne out of their innate love and respect for nature.

Forest has ever played a vital role in Khasi economy. Shifting cultivation, which is locally called 'Thang shyrti', is a forest-based method of cultivation followed by the Khasis since time immemorial. *Jhum* cultivation with all its demerits and adverse opinions has come to stay in Khasi society even to this day because it is labour intensive and abound in socio-cultural ethos. In Lawbyrwa, a sample village of this study, 60 per cent of the adult working population are found engaged in forest related activities, 23.89 per cent in small industry like carpentry, cane and bamboo works, etc. The land use pattern of the village shows that the major portion of 53.85 per cent of the land is used for forest, 19.23 per cent for *jhum* cultivation and a negligible 3.85 per cent of the land used for settled cultivation. The study conducted in this village reveals that the economy of the village is largely based on forest with majority of men, women and children engaged in cutting firewood, making charcoal, collecting and selling wild vegetables, bamboo shoot, mushroom, etc. Agriculture is the mainstay of the Khasis which is essentially based on agro-forestry. The land is communally owned and anyone is free to occupy and cultivate the land for which he need not pay. Thus, it reveals to us a picture of very high dependency of the life, culture and economy on the natural resources and environment.

The village Madan Ïing Syiem, though not a forested village as Lawbyrwa, represents a similar situation of dependency on forest produces like timber, firewood, bamboo and thatch. However, in recent years due to pressure of population, people have gradually drifted away from their traditional economic pursuit but socially and culturally they continue to make use of forest products in their daily life. The use of fuelwood as a source of household energy has been one of the major requirements of the people of this village. Data collected shows that out of a sample of 60 households, a total 100 per cent, i.e. all the households use firewood as a primary source of energy mainly for cooking, heating, drying and warming during winter. However, the requirements of firewood and charcoal are met with from outside the village. They are therefore, sold at a high price—each splitted piece of firewood weighing about 1kg costing Rs. 3 and charcoal Rs. 10 per kg. Thus, Khasi tradition has its impact deep-rooted so as the rising prices not being able to dislodge it.

The existence of Village forest on the outskirt of the village Madan Ïing Syiem and commonly held by four surrounding villages is yet another indication of the sense of expediency of the Khasis about the traditional usages of forest. Inspite of changes in the livelihood of the people and scarcity of land, the villagers still maintain the village forest for the benefit of the community as a whole. This fact goes to confirm the continuity of Khasi linkage with nature and environment which they have nurtured well till today.

It is important to note that though the advent of Christianity and the flow of Western culture have not affected the cultural fulcrum of the Khasi society as a whole, it has somehow alienated them from certain ritualistic aspects of forest usages. However, 'forest' continues to be intimately connected to the life and economy of the Khasis till recent times and it has continued to play its multidimensional uses in their life.

There has been an Infringement on People's Traditional Rights over Forest

The advent of the British colonial rule may be seen as a watershed in the ecological history of Khasi and Jaintia Hills. The rights and privileges over the natural forest and environment enjoyed by the Khasis in the past centuries were not to be as such for long. The British, through the enactment of forest laws and regulations for the first time in the history of tribal land, introduced statutory interference on the traditional usage of the free gifts of nature. As pointed out by Madhav Gadgil and Ramachandra Guha, "Colonialism's most tangible outcome some of whose effects persists to this day is related to its global control of resources." (Gadgil and Guha, 1992:116)

It is a well established fact that State control over forests has systematically eroded people's traditional rights over natural resources thus posing a threat not only to their livelihood but also to the delicate balance between tribals and the forest.

In the present study, this situation has largely been the outcome of the following two factors:

- Forest for revenue.
- Forest for development.

Forest for Revenue

The British created State forests and scientifically organised them as a profit making enterprise. The Indian Forest Act 1865, sought to create a class of Government protected forest. Thereafter, the Indian Forest Act 1878 was passed where two categories of state owned forests—'Reserved Forest' and 'Protected Forest' came into existence, with the prime intention of supplying timber to industrial sectors and to earn revenue for the State. Forests were since then seen as a revenue-yielding property, which could be commercially exploited. Obviously, the objectives of these Acts were to define the legal status and extent of proprietary rights of the Government in the forest.

The Reserved Forests were not intended as popularly believed for producing timber for public use but for meeting the requirement of the state. The legal provisions created by the laws to restrict people's usages were mainly designed on revenue earning motive rather than on social or environmental considerations. That the imperatives of colonial forestry were essentially commercial and not environmental was amply clarified when the most valuable timber 'Teak' grown in India was exported to England for use by the Royal Navy in ship building during Anglo-French War of early 19th century. The 'Sal', another hard and durable variety of timber was extensively used for railway sleepers and factory purposes. As the railway expansion and establishment of tea gardens started growing, the increased demand for timber led to the enactment of the Indian Forest Act, 1878 which further strengthened the grip of the Government over the natural forest resources of entire Northeast regions. More and more areas of forested land came under the Reserved and Protected forests resulting in increasing legal infringement on the traditional rights of the people over their natural resources. In 1927, Indian Forest Act, XVI came into operation superceding all other existing laws and regulations which lasted as the supreme statutory provisions regulating all forest administrations for the rest of the British rule till Independence of India.

The statistics maintained by the Forest Department shows that from the very first year they earned a revenue of Rs. 64,749. Thereafter, as the years passed by the forest revenue shot up steadily to Rs. 379,448 in 1889-90 and Rs. 568,100 in 1890-1900 (A.C. Sinha, 1993:145). Large areas of forest coups comprising matured trees were systematically demarcated and auctioned out to timber contractors for operation and pale in the markets as per rules set for the purpose. With the expansion of tea plantation in the North East demand for timber grew up. A number of saw mills and subsidiary industries for producing plywood for making tea chests sprang up around forest reserves. Supply of railway sleepers to Assam Bengal Railway and Eastern Bengal Railways, which were engaged in extension of new railway lines in the Northeast, contributed a major source of income to the State. It contributed nearly 60 per cent revenue to the total of forest income in the year 1912. The Second World War witnessed another spate of demand for forest materials for construction of military barracks, temporary quarters and bridges. Contractors had brisk business during early 1940s in supplying bamboo and timber with the help of bamboo rafts flowing down the Brahmaputra River.

The hill districts of Assam, inspite of transport bottlenecks, were not spared. Large quantities for timber logs, bamboo and other forest products found their ways through rivers, elephant and human labour.

During this long period of British rule a considerable area of forested land of Khasi and Jaintia Hills which were clad with rich forest and natural vegetation were brought under legal ownership of the British Government, depriving the tribal forest dwellers of their natural rights. According to an estimate the land converted into Reserved and Protected forests in Khasi and Jaintia Hills amounted to 427.79 sq. km., which is certainly a large area for a small hill district. An area of 590 acres was based in 1871-72 at the annual rent of Rs. 150 from the hills situated around Shillong for the purpose of timber plantation. According to record available with the Government of Meghalaya, in 1885 Riat Laban and Shyrwat forests were constituted into Reserved Forests, in 1889 Short Round, Upper Shillong and Laitkor Green Blocks were created as Protected Forests and in 1892 Riatkhwan was constituted into Reserved Forests. Another two big areas were converted into Reserved Forest from Jaintia Hills namely, Saipung in 1887 and Narpuh in 1909. For an average Khasi farmer who depended heavily on *Jhum* cultivation as his livelihood and collected his daily necessities of life from the forests, the conversion of these vast natural resources into state property not only told upon their tribal economy but also on their tradition and cultural heritage.

The Reserved Forests created by British Government through the process of law was no forest in the true sense of the tribal concept. The people could see no meaning in the so-called forest where they could not enter and cut down a branch of a tree and could not utilise its produce. For a tribal, the land and the forest are free gifts of nature and they belong to the community for the common benefit of all. It was, therefore, natural on the part of the indigenous people to feel resented against the conversion of their tribal land and forests into the Reserved and Protected forests restricting the use of its flora and fauna. Although the illiterate and innocent villagers could not raise any organised resistance against this injustice meted out to them, some sporadic uprising of the people was not at all lacking. The voice raised by one lakh Garos in February 1906 against reservation of forest in Garo Hills under the leadership of Sonaram Sangma is a case in point. In their petition they claimed that "their ancestors had enjoyed the privilege of living in forest in Garo Hills, made use of the forest products, sold them for their benefits besides cultivating and having rights of pastorage" (Sinha, 1993:45).

Forest for Development

The process of economic development that followed after successive implementation of various development programmes during the post-independence period brought about another wave of pressure on the land and natural resources of the country. Large-scale economic growth, mushroom growth of industries, increase in population, urbanisation, infrastructural development through expansion of roads and rails, buildings and parks, etc. resulted in the increased demand for raw materials like timber, bamboo, coal, limestone and other forest products. The forest situation during post-Independence period is no better. Immediately after Independence the Government of India adopted the National Forest Policy in 1952, which envisaged expansion of forest cover to one-third of the country's geographical area and in case of hill states and territories to 60 per cent of the total area of the state or territory. This policy gave a new thrust to the colonial forest expansionists policy and brought additional areas of land under forest cover through implementation of various schemes under Five Year Plans such as Social Forestry programme, afforestation drive, artificial regeneration programme, etc. The National Commission on Agriculture, 1976 recommended establishment of Forest Development Corporations in all states in order to undertake plantation activities and to carry out felling, processing and marketing of timber. The Commission also recommended drastic restrictions in people's access to forest and forest produce.

An important feature of post-Independent policy of India was rapid extension of agriculture operations through 'grow more food' programmes, which contributed to increase in agricultural land. In 1950-51 the area under agriculture was 118 million hectares, which increased to 143 million hectares in 1973-79. This additional land comes from wasteland, grassland, hill slopes, etc. through the process of reclamation and development. Obviously, these lands were the part of fallow lands where the tribals carried out *jhum* cultivation and were left temporarily fallow for vegetation to grow. The net result, therefore, was reduction in the land for *jhum* cultivation. In this connection, a report published by the Director of Economics and Statistics, Ministry of Agriculture and Irrigation, Government of India makes a significant revelation. The report states that during the period from 1972 to 1988 there is an increase in the area under forest in Meghalaya by 3.10 per cent and under agriculture by 1.78 per cent, on the other hand there is a corresponding decrease in the area under cultivable waste and pasture grassland by 8.90 per cent and 1.50 per cent respectively. This increase in the areas under forest and agriculture with corresponding decrease in the area under cultivable waste and pasture grassland undoubtedly suggests consequent deprivation of that much of *jhum* land to tribal *jhumias*. The Forest Conservation Act 1980 restricted the State Governments from conversion of any forest land into non-forest purposes meaning thereby that any further requirement of land for other development purposes like construction of roads, buildings, dams, stadias, fisheries, orchards, etc. has to be met from cultivable wasteland, pastures, jungles or vegetation etc. which again are the lands where *jhum* cultivation is carried out.

Our planners found in the hills, tremendous potentialities for development of various mineral and forest based industries with inexhaustible strove of natural wealth. Numerous saw mills, plywood factories, cement factories, coal mines, carpentry and cane and bamboo workshops and paper mills grew up in an around Meghalaya. The course of development that took place during the next few decades left a deep scar on the green landscape of Meghalaya and almost dismantled its eco-system.

A Satellite Imagery Survey Report of 1994 showed that Meghalaya lost 106 sq. km. (10,600 ha.) of forest cover during the last two years, i.e. 1992 and 1993 (D. Pyngrope *et al.*, 1994:4). The Chief Conservator of Forest (Forest and Environment) of Meghalaya admitted that about 6000 hectares of state's woodland area was subjected to felling for commercial or otherwise use, resulting in extraction of 2 to 3 lakhs cubic metres of timber every year on average (Apphira, Jan. 3, 1995).

The people of village Lawbyrwa are the case in point who lost their *jhum* land for construction of Umiam Hydro-Electric Project, one of the biggest power projects of the North-East. In 1959-68, the Assam State Electricity Board acquired a vast stretch of cultivable land from Lawbyrwa village measuring four square miles for construction of a massive water reservoir and a Power House including office buildings, workshop and staff quarters. No substitute lands were provided to the landowners who lost their lands and compensation was paid after several years of dispossession of the land. From the data collected during field study it is seen that as many as 50 per cent of the villagers of Lawbyrwa are marginal farmers with land holdings less than 5 acres each and 20 per cent of them are landless cultivators. These landless farmers either cultivate other's land on crop-sharing basis or engage themselves in non-agricultural activities as daily labourers. Present study shows that 11.11 per cent of the people of this village etc. eke their livelihood by working as daily labourers. It sounds paradoxical to find landlessness in the Khasi society where land belongs to the community and every member of the society has the right to possess and cultivate land. But it is a harsh reality today.

The diarchical form of control and management of forest in Meghalaya by the State Forest Department and the Autonomous District Councils has contributed to dual forest policies, lack of co-ordination and division of accountability. Both the authorities formulate their own forest policies and follow a separate set of forest rules and regulations in their respective areas of operation. The main reason for such a diarchy is that, while the State Forest Department maintains a well-qualified team of skilled technical staff, it has a comparatively meagre area of 1127.23 sq.km of forest under its jurisdiction. (Statistical details given in Appendix III) The District Council on the other hand, has a large forest cover of 6250.68 sq.km under its management and control and yet it suffers from inadequate technical manpower, which has resulted in the lack of enforcement of rules.

Forest being the principal source of revenue the District Councils could not afford to stop forest operation under prevailing fund constraints. The private forest owners who own substantial areas of forests indulged freely in sale of timber from their forests. According to the United Khasi and Jaintia Hills Autonomous District (Management and Control of Forest) Act, 1958, the private forests in Meghalaya are under the control and supervision of the District Council Authorities, but in reality, the private owners think themselves free to operate in these forests. Larger quantity of timber than what Meghalaya consumed found their ways to Assam and other states. The Acts and legislation passed by the State for conservation of forests, protection of catchment areas, and prohibition of felling and removal of timber, etc. had very little effect until the Supreme Court intervened with a blanket ban on logging timber in December 1996.

Looking closely at the above two perspectives of forest utilization viz. Forest for revenue and Forest for development, which have led to infringement of people's traditional rights over forest, it is seen that they have had a serious impact on people's livelihood thereby conflicting on their traditional rights over forest resources.

Forest for Livelihood

The Autonomous District Council has classified these forest products as "minor", as it gives little revenue to it, but for a Khasi, minor forest products form a major source of income. According to Khasi Hills Autonomous District (Management and Control of Forest-revised rates of royalty) Rules 1984, the minor forest product includes Tezpatta, firewood, agarwood, broomstick, charcoal, thatch, bamboo, fodder grass, wild pepper, sisia bark (*Cinnamomum zelanicum*), etc. This means that practically all kinds of natural resources growing the forest, except commercial timber are classified as minor forest products, which constitute the most essential items of everyday use of the tribals. More than timber, it is the above-mentioned minor forest products which play a crucial role in supporting the life of the tribal community in the shape of subsidiary source of income generation. In Lawbyrwa it is found that 17.22 per cent of its population are engaged in collecting and selling of minor forest products like wild vegetables, tubers, bamboo shoots and edible fruits etc. Firewood and charcoal are indispensable sources of energy used in every Khasi household for cooking, heating and drying purposes. Data collected from Lawbyrwa village shows that 20.56 per cent of adult workers are engaged in cutting and selling firewood and 22.22 per cent of them eke out their livelihood by making and selling charcoal. The provisions of existing forest rules of Meghalaya claim that all forest produce irrespective of major or minor legally belong to the State and removal of any of the product is illegal and punishable as per rules. The Section 5 of the United Khasi and Jaintia Hills Autonomous District (Management and Control of Forest) Act 1958 lays down that "No timber or forest produce shall be removed for the purpose of sale, trade or business from the protected forests, Green Blocks, Unclassed forests and Reserved forests without order in writing of the Forest Officer of the District Council." Thus, the State and the Autonomous District Councils have systematically appropriated and commercialised the forest resources depriving the Khasis of the benefit from the minor forest products, and with this the indigenous people stand completely alienated from their community land, the timber fuelfood and fodder. According to records available from the Khasi Hills Autonomous District Council, the revenue collected from minor forest products during the last five years from 2001 to 2005 was Rs. 75,45,970 which comes to Rs. 15,09,194 per year on an average. This shows the volume of income generated by the minor forest produces of Khasi Hills which would have otherwise gone to the dependents had it not been appropriated by the District Council.

According to Khasi Land Tenure System, there are two categories of land, namely, *Ri Raid* or Community land and *Ri-Kynti* or Private land. The former category of land is set aside for the use of the community over which each Khasi member of the village has the right of use and occupancy. But he has no right to inheritance or transfer of the land. His occupancy right lasts as long as he uses the land for himself and his family, but his right terminates if he fails to utilise the said land for three consecutive years and the land reverts back to the community. However, if he has made any permanent improvement over the land or raises any structure or permanent fencing around the plot of land it becomes his permanent property as *Ri Kynti* land. This loophole present in the Khasi land tenure system offers an incentive to many people to convert *Ri Raid* land into their private property as *Ri Kynti* land. Persons with wisdom and ability could through application of labour and capital establish durable assets or *Ri Raid* land and claim the same as their individual possession at the cost of the community. This process of converting community land into private land has come a long way taking the advantage of Government grant-in-aid and loans under various development schemes like social forestry, fishery and farming. Today vast areas of *Ri Raid* land all over Khasi Hills have been transformed into farmlands, fishery ponds, orchards, forest land, etc. The socio-economic implication of this trend is all too apparent, as it has led to gradual diminishing of cultivable community land and vegetations where the people had easy access to their necessities of life. There is no knowing as to how much of the *Ri Raid* land has been converted into *Ri Kynti* land or how much unclassed forest area has been brought under Reserved forest and protected forest because of the fact that in Khasi Hills no land has been surveyed and cadestral record prepared except for Government land. This is another serious loose end of the Khasi land tenure system. Thus, it is seen that there is a process of gradual privatisation of community land and concentration of the basic means of production in the hand of a few people who pose as landlords and moneylenders.

Thus, it is apparent that, "Land" and "Forest" being the natural productive resources at the base, there is an emerging conflict between the State and the people over the rights to land and its natural products ever since the advent of colonial rule in India to the present time. Inspired by the ideals of nation building as upheld by the Constitution the Government of India forgot about the tender man-nature relationship that existed in the tribal areas. During the past few decades the state increasingly overstepped in its forest policies in the tribal land in respect of both control and utilisation of the forest resources. Needless to say that the most affected by these policies were the forest dwellers who lived in the villages. The study has ample evidences to show that the State control of forest and enactment of Forest Acts and rules over the years have not only infringed into the people rights over the minor forest produce but also contributed to depletion of natural forest resources. The process has led to a number of untraditional economic phenomena like decline in shifting cultivation, transition from forest based economy to open and diversified economy, concentration of land in the hands of certain group of people, landlessness, share-cropping etc. which cannot be termed as positive indication of development.

The Inevitable Shift

The facts and circumstances discussed above lead us to the conclusion that there is a gradual and inevitable shift in the pattern of Khasi livelihood from a traditional forest-based economy to a modern, open and more diversified means of living. There is a visible transition in Khasi society with regard to the state of their dependence on forest resources like food, fodder and shelter to other means of living. The depletion of land and natural forest cover, which were their only economic base, resulted in the paucity of forest land for *jhum* cultivation. Pressure of population on existing land aggravated the situation and reduced *jhum* cycle period from 15-20 years to 3-5 years resulting in degeneration of *jhum* land and low productivity. The *jhumia* families gradually turned to settled cultivation or *Bun* cultivation, an alternative method of *jhum* cultivation. According to a report of the State Soil Conservation Department there was 27.04 per cent decline in the number of households dependant on *jhum* during the past 30 years from 1971 to 2001. In Lawbyrwa 19.23 per cent of the land was used for *jhum* cultivation and 3.85 per cent for settled cultivation while in the village Madan Ïing Syiem 15.24 per cent land was under settled cultivation and no land was used for *jhum* cultivation.

The conversion of natural forests and wastelands into Reserved forest, Protected and Unclassed forests by the State and Autonomous District Councils led to increased restrictions on tribal access to forests, rivers and fisheries, etc. The plethora of forest laws and regulations enacted by the authorities in the name of development of forest and environment severely infringed the tribal rights to natural forests and forest produces.

On the other hand, a change in the economic pursuit is well reflected in the village Madan Ïing Syiem. This is an old Khasi village of greater Mylliem village, which was once a centre of Khasi culture and tradition. Iron smelting and export of iron to Sylhet was its traditional industry, which has become extinct today due to its primitive and unscientific method of processing and also because of the thin forest cover in the village. This is evident from the field data, which shows that except for the privately owned patches of forest, the overall forest cover in the village is *nil*. The total area under forest cover in this village is only 10 acres (4.76%) as against a total land area of 210 acres, which is why, local felling of trees even for firewood and household requirements is totally prohibited today. A sizeable section of the inhabitants i.e., 37.11 per cent are engaged in various trade and business, cottage industry and Government services while less than half of the working adults, i.e., 40 per cent still carryout agriculture of which some as secondary occupation. A striking feature of the economy is that not a single household is engaged in forest activities for its livelihood. There is no *Ri Raid* (community) land, all lands are *Ri Kynti* (Private) land and there is no practice of *jhum* cultivation. They have taken to settled cultivation.

Recently, The Scheduled Tribes (Recognition of Forest Rights) Bill 2005 was formulated by the Indian Ministry of Tribal Affairs to affirm the land rights of India's forest dwelling tribal people. The Bill seeks to recognise rights to forest produce, intellectual property and traditional knowledge, while also conferring duties on the Scheduled Tribes and acknowledging the close connection between the well being of the forest dwellers and the health of the eco-system. However, the Forest Rights Bill has been criticised by the Ministry of Environment and Forests, which argues that the Bill will hinder efforts to preserve India's dwindling forest cover, cause irreparable ecological damage. Social groups are also concerned that the Bill will harm the livelihood of forest dwellers who are not considered to be part of Scheduled Tribes. Thus, the Bill in its present form is bogged by controversy with many social and conservation groups as also the Ministry of Environment and Forest (MoEF) opposing it. In response to these concerns, the Indian Cabinet has suspended discussion of the Bill until it receives comments from members of the public. Nonetheless, the drafting of the Forest Rights Bill, which explicitly recognises historical and social injustice, as a serious and legitimate concern, represents a significant step towards the recognition of forest dweller rights in India. The Union Minister for Development of North-East Region has recently converted a draft National Tribal Policy with a view to addressing issues like enhancement of human development index of tribals, ensuring their control over natural resources and distribution of wealth and opportunities among the tribals who are hitherto deprived of them (*Shillong Times*, dt. 24-7-2006).

Appendix-I

List of Plants and Herbs which Begin with the Prefix '*JA*'

1. Jakhria (*Rhynchotechum ellipticum*)
2. Jalyngiar (*Sunchus arvensis*)
3. Jabuit (*Acanthaccae; Phlo goganthus gamflei*)
4. Jalyngkthem saw
5. Jalyngab lieh (*Astecaceae; Senecio densiflorus*)
6. Jalyngnap iong (*Asteracaea; Inula cappa*)
7. Jaskei
8. Jamiaw
9. Jamiaw madan
10. Jathang
11. Jatira
12. Jada dieng
13. Jada hati
14. Jada shnong
15. Jathynrait rilum
16. Jathynrait riwar
17. Jasnian
18. Jatung
19. Jarasong
20. Jalynsiang
21. Jatangniang
22. Jarain
23. Jakhain (*Asteracsae; Pieris hieraciodes*)
24. Jakhain pakhama (*Asteraceae Hypocharis*)
25. Jarem
26. Jarem saw
27. Jarem Shrieh

28. Jahynwet
29. Jaralud
30. Jali
31. Jali Sniang
32. Jali Krem
33. Jali Pnar
34. Jalynteng
35. Jalwain iong
36. Japri
37. Jasniang
38. Jalyngiem
39. Jawer
40. Janailar
41. Janailar Phud
42. Jalu
43. Jarumshiah (*Zehneri heterophylla*)
44. Jashun (*Verbanaceae ruvella*)
45. Jahynlaw (*Viburnum cariaceum*)
46. Jaiur
47. Jaiur jhur
48. Jaiur khlam
49. Jalynnoh
50. Jalynnoh skei
51. Jadaw
52. Jalyngbien
53. Japung
54. Japung ktieh
55. Jaler
56. Jalmut
57. Jalmut shniuh
58. Jamynsleh
59. Jamyrwai
60. Ka Jamynrei
61. Jamyrwait rit sla
62. Jamynrei ritbian
63. Jajew skei
64. Jakrai
65. Jakrai Lum

66. Japongdung
67. Jalyniar prohsla
68. Jamyrdoh
69. Jangew
70. Jalkhan Lieh
71. Jalkhan iong
72. Jalkhan heh
73. Jalyngkhan
74. Jaltham
75. Jawieh raij
76. Jalieh dymmiew
77. Japu
78. Jakba
79. Jalong
80. Jamiyiang
81. Jamiyiang synrai (*Ternstomoceae; Camellia sp. F. Theaceae*)
82. Jashiah
83. Jaler lum
84. Jakhaw shoin
85. Jashun
86. Japri
87. Japri lum
88. Jajew shilliang
89. Jajew shyrtong syiar
90. Jajew saw
91. Jajer
92. Jawieh
93. Jawieh
94. Jaum
95. Jalynnoh skei
96. Jalbuit
97. Ja Dieng Janai
98. Jating
99. Japiur
100. Japiur iong
101. Jasat
102. Jakhi iong
103. Jakhi shniuh

104. Jakhi rit
105. Jakhi nuli
106. Jaiing
107. Jalyngap sohriewlong
108. Jalyngap shymprong
109. Jarsang
110. Jasar
111. Janei
112. Jaryndem
113. Japang (*Probila' denticulate*)

Source: S. Khongsit, 1999. Kiba Ngi Khot Ja, *Shillong: Mrs. Sucila Khongngain, San Mer.*

Appendix-II

List of Species of Bamboo that are Locally Grown in the Khasi Hills

Sl. No.	*Local Names*	*Botanical Names*
1.	U Tangei	
2.	U Namlong	*Chimonobambusa khasiana*
3.	U Stew	
4.	U Stew Ïong	
5.	U Spit	
6.	U Sylli	*Cephalo satchyum pallisium*
7.	U Tmar	
8.	U Dongla	
9.	U Shlu	
10.	U Spar Khlaw	*Bambusa grififithi*
11.	U Spar Bah	
12.	U Spar Ïong	
13.	U Spar Lum	
14.	U Spar Naha	
15.	U Sba	
16.	U Sba Heh	
17.	U Siej Naka	*Phylostechyus manü*
18.	U Tyr-a Riwar	*Cephalo stashyum cepilatum*
19.	U Tyr-a Bhoi	*Dendrodavanauios*
20.	U Muri	
21.	U Rñai	
22.	U Rñai shilot	
23.	U Rñai Ïong	
24.	U Pautabat	
25.	U Rthem	

26.	U Shken	*Dendocalamus hamiltonii*
27.	U shken Ïong	
28.	U Tanglar	
29.	U Tawang Ïong	
30.	U Siej Lieh	
31.	U Siej Saw	
32.	U Siej Ïong	
33.	U Siej Buid	
34.	U Siej Smit	
35.	U Siej Tyrkhaw	
36.	U Siej Naka Ïong	
37.	U Siej Jympun	
38.	U Siej Stem	
39.	U Siej Makar	
40.	U Latuba	
41.	U Siej Thohrew	
42.	U Siej Makar	
43.	U Siej Khongpong	

Source: S. Khongsit, 1999. Hangne Tang Ïa U Siej, *Shillong: Mrs. Sucila Khongngain, San Mer.*

Appendix-III

Forest Areas Directly under the Control of the State Forests, Department of Meghalaya

(a) Reserved Forests	712.15 sq.kms.
(b) Protected Forests	12.39 sq.kms.
(c) National Parks	399.482 sq.kms.
(d) Proposed Nonumiang & Gittingri Reserved Forests	2.71 sq.kms.
(e) Areas under Parks & Gardens	0.50 sq.kms.
Total-A	**1127.232 sq.kms.**
(f) Forest areas in the campus of the North-Eastern Hills University	3 sq.kms. (approx.)
(g) Forest areas under Defence	4 sq.kms. (approx.)
Total-B	**7 sq.kms. (approx.)**

2. Forest Areas under the Control of the Autonomous District Councils

A. Jaintia Hills Autonomous District Council

(a) Unclassed State Forests	1000 sq.kms. (approx.)
(b) Protected Forests	34.22 sq.kms. (approx.)
(c) Village Reserved Forests	3.49 sq.kms.
(d) Private/Community Forests	Extent of the area not known at present since survey records are not available
Total-C	**1037.71 sq.kms. (approx.)**

Appendix-V

Area which are Forests Irrespective of whether They are so Notified Recognised for Classified under any Law and Irrespective of the Ownership of the Land of such Forest

A. Forest Areas Directly Under the Control of the State Department, Meghalaya

Name of Reserved Forests	Gazette Notification and Date	Area (sq.kms.)
1. Saipung Reserved Forests	No. 26/8/1876 & 5 of 17.10.1877	150.35
2. Narpuh Block I	No. 3978 F of 17.6.1809	62.42
3. Narpuh Block II	No. 1106 R of 9.3.1918	98.68
4. Riat Khwan Reserved Forest	No. 806 R of 5.3.1892 and 4287 R of 1.9.1892	3.91
5. Shyrwat Reserved Forest	No. F or 179/80/187 of 28.3.1988	0.44
6. Riat Laban Reserved Forest	No. F or 179/80/183 of 28.3.1988	2.05
7. Nongkhyllem Reserved Forest	No. 4692 F of 23.7.1909 and 864 G-J of 4.2.1939	125.91
8. Umsaw Reserved Forest	No. G.F.R. 234/46/3 of 16.12.1946	0.44
9. Chymabongshi Reserved Forest	No. 28 dt. 19.6.1883 and FOR/SECTT/492/63/4 dt.22.12.1965	23.28
10. Dhima Reserved Forest	No. 28 dt.19.6.1983 and 3751 R of 11.8.1904	20.72
11. Rajasimla Reserved Forest	No. 28 of 19.6.1983 and 665 R of 15.2.1899	18.13
12. Dilma Reserved Forest	No. 28 of 19.6.1883	2.59
13. Dildek Reserved Forest	No. 28 of 19.6.1883	2.59
14. Darugiri Reserved Forest	No. 28 of 19.6.1883 and 365 R of 29.1.1932	10.36
15. Rongrengiri Reserved Forest	No. 28 of 19.6.1883 and 375 R of 29.1.1932	36.26

(*Contd.*)

(*Contd.*)

Name of Reserved Forests	Gazette Notification and Date	Area (sq.kms.)
16. Dambu Reserved Forest	No. 22 of 12.3.1880 and 4276 R of 14.10.1962	18.13
17. Songsak Reserved Forest	No. 29 of 1.10.1885 and 3583 R of 5.9.1902	23.31
18. Dilbru Hills Reserved Forest	No. 28 dt. 19.6.1883 and 3526 R of 10.12.1930	15.02
19. Tura Peak Reserved Forest	No. FOR/10/75/32 dt. 23.6.1982	4.19
20. Baghmara Reserved Forest	No. 12 dt. 24.2.1887 (1.40 dereserved vide G.O.I. L/No. 8-98/81-FRY (COORD) dt.14.5.1982	43.91
21. Angratoli Reserved Forest	No. 3 dt. 7.11.1883 and 1699 R of 26.7.1932	30.11
22. Rawat Reserved Forest	No. 44 dt. 7.11.1883 and 1699 R of 26.7.1932	6.47
23. Emangiri Reserved Forest	No. 44 dt. 7.1.1883 and 1699 R of 26.7.1932	8.29
24. Siju Reserved Forest	No. 44 dt. 7.11.1883 and 2323 R of 26.7.1932	5.18
Total Reserved Forest		**712.15**
1. Nongumiang	Area acquired and step being taken for declaring as a Reserved Forest	0.31
2. Gittingiri	Area obtained in exchange of 140 ha. of Baghmara Reserved Forest vide GOI L/No. 8-89/81/FRY (COORD) dt. 14.5.1982. Area is being declared as a Reserved Forest	2.40
Total Area being proposed as Reserved Forest		**2.71**

Source: Forest Department, Government of Meghalaya.

Appendix-VI

List of some Important Timbers Found in Meghalaya

	Local (Common) Name	Commercial Name	Botanical Name
1.	Dieng Soh Risang	Indian Horn Beams	*Carpinus vaminea*
2.	Tik, Teak, Segun	Teak	*Tectona grandis*
3.	Dieng Laphiang, gippok,	Gamari. Bol Gamari	*Gmelina arborea*
4.	Dieng Rai,	Tita Sopa	*Champ Michelia champaca*
5.	Bola, Dieng Bilat, Bolsen	Bola	*Morus laevigata*
6.	Nahar Dieng Ngai	Mesua	*Mesua ferrea*
7.	Sal, Dieng Blei, Bol Sal	Sal	*Shorea robusta*
8.	Mundhani	Mundani	*Acrocarpus fraxinifalius*
9.	Amari, Lali	Amari	*Amoora wallichii*
10.	Cham,	Sam	*Artocarpus Chaplasha*
11.	Birch, Dieng Lieng	Birch	*Betula alnoides*
12.	Bogipoma, Diengbt, Tyrneng,	Bol	*Derek Chikrassia Chikrassia tabularis*
13.	Khokan, Dieng Bai Lampati	Khokan	*Duabangagrandiflora*
14.	Karal	Karal	*Kayea floribunda*
15.	Badam	Badam	*Mansonia dipikai*
16.	Holok, Diengmaras Rakseng	Hollock	*Terminalia myriocarpa*
17.	Poma, Dieng Bti	Toon	*Toona ciliata*
18.	Kadam	Kadam	*Anthocephalus cadamba*
19.	Pine, Khasi Pine, Kseh	Pine	*Pinus kesiya*
20.	Gogra, Dieng Ngan	Gogra/Chilauni	*Schima khasianal*

Appendix-VII

National Parks and Sanctuaries

	Name of Parks/Sanctuaries	Gazette Notification and Date	Area (sq.kms.)
1.	Bhalphakram National Park	No. FOR. 103 34/354 dt.15.2.1986	220.00
2.	Bhalphakram National Park	Area acquired but yet to be notified as National Park	132.00*
3.	Nokrek National Park	No. FOR. 23/86/204 dt. 29.11.1986	47.48
Total National Parks			**399.482**
* Area already acquired but yet to be notified as National Park			
Sanctuaries			
1.	Nongkhyllem Wild Life Sanctuary	No. FOR. 25/81/5 dt.25.3.1981	29.00
2.	Siju Wild Life Sanctuary	No. MFG. 66/4 dt.30.3.1981	5.18
3.	Baghmara Pitcher Plant Sanctuary	No. FOR. 79/84/5 dt.24.5.1984	0.02
Total Sanctuaries			**34.20**
Area included in Reserved Forests			
C. Protected Forests			
1.	Upper Shillong Protected Forests		7.88
2.	Short Round Protected Forests		1.13
3.	Laitkor Protected Forests		3.25
4.	Umkhuti Protected Forests		0.14
5.	Green Block No. 2		0.21
Total Protected Forests			**12.39**
Reserved Forests			712.15
Protected Forests			12.39
National Parks			399.482
			1124.022
Nongumiang and Gittingiri Proposed Reserved Forests			**2.71**
Grand Total			**1126.732**

Source: Forest Department, Government of Meghalaya.

Bibliography

Agarwal, Anil, 1992. 'The Price of Forests', *Proceedings of a Seminar on the Economics of the Sustainable Use of Forest Resources*. New Delhi: Centre for Science and Environment,

Allen, B.C., 1980. *Gazetteer of the Khasi and Jaintia Hills, Garo Hills, Lushai Hills*. New Delhi: Gyan Publications.

Arnold, David and Guha, Ramchandra (eds.). 1996. *Nature, Culture, and Imperialism: Essays on the environmental History of South Asia*. Delhi: Oxford University Press.

Arnold, David, 1996. *The Problem of Nature*. UK: Blackwell Publishers.

Apphira Daily News, Vol. III, No. 83. Shillong, dt. May 14, 1997.

Bareh, Hamlet, 2001. *The Economy of Meghalaya: Tradition to Transition*, Guwahati: Spectrum Publications.

Barpujari, H K. 1992. *The Comprehensive History of Assam* (Vols. III, IV and V) Guwahati: Spectrum Publications.

Centre for Science and Environment, 1985. 'The State of India's Environment 1984-85: A Second Citizen's Report'. New Delhi: Centre for Science and Environment.

Chaudhuri, Budhadeb and Maiti, Ashok Kumar, 1986. *Forest and Forest Development in India*. New Delhi: Inter India Publications.

Chaudhury, J.N., 1978. *The Khasi Canvas*. Shillong: Smt. Jaya Chaudhury.

Choube, S.K., *Hill Politics in North East,* 1973, Orient Longman, Patna.

Darlong, V.T., 2002, 'An Overview of Forest Policies and Legislations *vis-à-vis* Forest Resource Management in North-East India' in B. Datta Ray & K. Alam (ed.). *Forest Resources in North East India*. New Delhi: Omson Publications.

Dutta, B.B. and Karna, M.N., 1987. *Land Relations in North East India*, New Delhi: People's Publishing House.

Evans, Julian, 2001. *The Forests Handbook.* (Vol. I). London: Blackwell Science Ltd.

FSI. 1989, 1997, 2001. 'The State of Forests Report 1989'. Dehradun: Forest Survey of India.

Gadgil, Madhav and Guha, Ramchandra, 1992. *This Fissured Land, An Ecological History of India.* Delhi: Oxford University Press.

Gopalakrishnan, R., 1995. *Meghalaya: Land and People*, New Delhi: Omsons Publications.

Government of Meghalaya, 2001, 'District Level Key Statistics Meghalaya, Shillong: Directorate of Economics and Statistics.

Government of Meghalaya, 1990-95. 'Eighth Five-Year Plan' (Vol. II) Shillong: Planning Department.

Government of Meghalaya, 2003. *Meghalaya: Socio-Economic Review*. Shillong: Directorate of Economics and Statistics.

Guha, Ramachandra and Gadgil, Madhav, January 1998. 'State Forestry and Social Conflict in British India: A Study in the Ecological Basis of Agrarian Protest' Technical Report, No. 51.

Guha, Ramachandra. 1983. 'Forestry in British and Post-British India: A Historical Analysis' *The Economic and Political Weekly*, 16(4): 18-25.

Guha, Ramachandra, 1994. *Social Ecology*. New Delhi: Oxford University Press.

Gurdon, P.R.T., 1975. *The Khasis*. Delhi: Cosmo Publications.

Handique, Rajib (2004), *British Forest Policy in Assam*, Concept Publishing, New Delhi.

Hardy, Thomas, 1920. *Under the Greenwood Tree*. London: Macmillan.

Jameson, A.K., quoted in S. Dasgupta (unpublished). 'The Local Face of Non-Cooperation: The Santhal Movement in Midnapur (1918-1923)'.

Kyndia, P.R., *Rev. JJM Nichols Roy: Architect of District Council Autonomy,* 1993, Sanchar Publishing House, New Delhi.

Lamin, Henry, 1995. *Economy and Society in Meghalaya*. New Delhi: Har Anand Publications.

Lenihan, John, 1975. *Environment and Man*, Glasgow: Blackie.

Lyngdoh, Mary Priscilla Rina, 1991. *The Festivals in the History and Culture of the Khasi*. New Delhi: Vikas Publishing House.

Mathew, T., 1980. *Tribal Economy of North-Eastern Region*. Gauhati: Spectrum Publications.

Mathur, P.R.G., 1979. *Khasi of Meghalaya*. Delhi: Cosmo Publications.

Mawrie, H.O., 1979. "God and Man" in *Khasi Heritage*. Shillong: Seng Khasi.

Mawrie, H.O., 1981. *The Khasi Milieu*. New Delhi: Concept Publishing Company.

Mawrie, L. Barnes, 2001. *The Khasis and their Natural Environment*. Shillong: Vendrame Institute Publication.

Mawthoh, P.R., 1984. "The Environmental Problems of Meghalaya" in I.J.S. Jaswal (ed.), *Status of Ecology*, Punjab: Punjab Publishing House.

Mukherjee, Anita Roy, 1995. *Forest Resources Conservation and Regeneration: A Study of West Bengal Plateau*. New Delhi: Concept Publishing Company.

Nongbri, Tiplut, 2003. *Development, Ethnicity and Gender: Select Essays on Tribes in India*. New Delhi: Rawat Publications.

Nongkynrih, A.K., 2000. *Human Development in Khatar Shnong*. Shillong: F. Nongkynrih.

Rawat, Ajay S., 1991. *History of Forestry in India*. New Delhi: Indus Publishing Company.

Ray, B. Datta and Alam, K., 2002. *Forest Resources in North East India*. New Delhi: Omsons Publications.

Regional Centre for Social Forestry and Wastelands Development, *Survival of Trees in Social Forestry Plantations of Meghalaya*, NEHU, Shillong, 1991.

Riordan, F.N.T.O., 1971. "Environmental Management: Progress in Geography".

Roy, Hipshon, 1979. *Khasi Heritage*. Shillong: Seng Khasi.

Rymbai, R.T., 1980. "Some Aspects of the Religion of the Khasi-Pnars" in Sujata Miri (ed.). *Religion and Society of North East India*. New Delhi: Vikas Publishing House Ltd.

Rymbai, T. *et al.*, 1974. "Report of the Land Reforms Commission", Government of Meghalaya, Shillong.

Sarma, Sidheswar, 2003. *Meghalaya the Land and Forest: A Remote Sensing Based Study*. Guwahati: Geophil Publishing House.

Semple, Ellen Churchill, 1911. Influence of Geographic Environment on the Basis of Ratzel's System of Anthro. Geography, London.

Sharma, B.D., 1978. "Forests, Tribal Economy and Regional Development", Tribal Research and Development Centre.

Sharma, B.D., 1978. "*Forests, Tribal Economy and Regional Development*", Tribal Research and Development Centre, Bhopal.

Shillong Times, Vol. IX, No. 97. Shillong, dt. July 24, 2006.

Simon, I.M., 1991. "Meghalaya District Gazetteers", Government of Meghalaya, Arts and Culture Department, Shillong.

Singh, Daman, 1996. "The Last Frontier—People and Forests in Mizoram", Tata Energy Research Institute, New Delhi.

Singh, G.B., 1987. *Forest Ecology of India*, Jaipur: Rawat Publications.

Sinha, A.C., 1988. "Forest Reservation and Movement for Its Dereservation Among the Garos" in *Social Science Probings*, March-December.

Sinha, A.C., 1993. *Beyond the Trees, Tigers and Tribes: Historical Sociology of the Eastern Himalayan Forests*. New Delhi: Har Anand Publications.

Sinha, A.C., 1994. *North-Eastern Frontier of India*. New Delhi: Indus Publishing Company.

Stebbing, E.P., 1982. *The Forests of India*, Vols. I, II and III. New Delhi: A.J. Printers Agency. First Published in 1926.

Stills, David, *International Encyclopaedia of Social Sciences, Vol. 5*. The Macmillan Company and the Free Press.

The United Khasi-Jaintia Hills Autonomous District (Management and Control of Forests) 1958, 1960 Acts and Rules, 1995. Shillong: Hills Autonomous District Council.

Tiwari, B.K. and Singh Surendra, 1995. *Eco-restoration of Degraded Hills*. Shillong: Kaushal Publications.

Tiwari, B.K. *et al.*, 1999. "Sacred Forests of Meghalaya", Regional Centre, National Afforestation and Eco-Development Board, NEHU, Shillong.

Vidyarthi, L.P. and Rai, B.K., 1976. *Tribal Culture of India*. New Delhi: Concept Publishing Company.

Voelkar, J.A., 1897. *Report on Indian Agriculture*, 2nd Edition, Calcutta.

Worster, D. (ed). 1998. "*The Ends of The Earth: Perspectives on Modern Environmental History*", Cambridge.

Vernacular Publications

Ka Theology Jong Ka Niam Khasi, 1990. Nongkrem: Kong Tmissilda Soh.

Khongsit, S., 1999. *Hangne Tang Ïa U Siej*. Shillong: Mrs. Sucila Khongngain, San Mer.

Khongsit, S., 1999. *Kiba Ngi Khot Ja*. Shillong: Mrs. Sucila Khongngain, San Mer.

Khongsit, S., 2001. *Ki Khlaw Ki Btap bad Ki Kam Ri Ngap*. Shillong: Mrs. Sucila Khongngain, San Mer.

Mawrie, H.O., 1972. *Ka Pyrkhat U Khasi*. Nongkrem: Kong Tmissilda Soh.

Ramsiej, K. Dhirendro, 1992. *Ka Mariang Ha U Khasi bad ki Purinam-Puriskam*. Shillong: Smti. I. Mylliem Nongpathaw. 1990 ka Theodogy Ing ka Niam Khasi. Nonghrem.

Index